We have entered

era in which the

meaning and

symbolism of

technology is

continuously

reinterpreted and

reassessed, and its

potential seems

to alternately

inspire and perplex.

An escalated urge
organic and the
one direction that
today's
when considering
and purpose of
in their work.

toward the
expressive is just
many of
architects take
the meaning
technology

Two works of residential architecture conceived in the first half of the twentieth century were pivotal in the later developments in the use of technology in architecture: Pierre Chareau's Maison de Verre in Paris (1928–32) and the Eames House (1945–49).

In a vastly different historical and ideological moment from that of mid-century, today's architectural culture permits and perhaps demands an expanded, inclusive sensibility shaped by the paradoxes of our own age, one that feeds upon past and present.

With the persistence of established presence Tech style, of a predominantly machined language in contemporary yet with

resurgence and

modernism and the

of the High-

numerous examples

structural,

can be discerned

architecture,

significant variations.

Whereas advances in technology and the machine have clearly had an impact on architecture, obvious technological engagement is only one of many communication devices available to architects.

Elizabeth A. T. Smith

Techno Architecture

With 324 illustrations, 115 in colour

Thames & Hudson

Contents

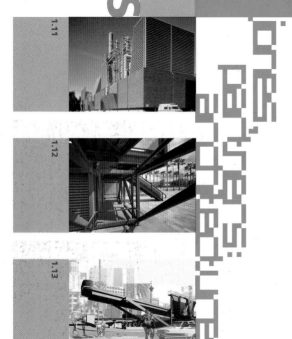

Introduction
The Culture of Technology

What is signified by the frank utilization of industrial materials, forms and imagery in American architecture today? Does it differ from the High-Tech approach of many predominantly European architects that first emerged in the 1960s and that has persisted over the last four decades? Is there a sensibility among a loose grouping of North American architects in current practice that reflects primarily a cultural, rather than functional or imagistic, commitment to the use of technology? This book considers such questions and presents and analyzes four architectural practices in whose work – some of the most compelling and exploratory today – the overt incorporation of technology is understood as a given.

With the resurgence and persistence of modernism and the established presence of the High-Tech style – a recognizable idiom based on articulation and amplification of production means in a building's components and systems – numerous examples of a predominantly structural, machined language can be discerned in contemporary architecture, yet with significant variations. Several writers have commented recently on a tendency toward hybridization and relaxation of the rigorously machined, even within the work of those architects who have been consistently identified with High Tech. For instance, John Welsh points to what he terms the 'technorganic' qualities of such buildings as Renzo Piano's Kansai International Airport (Osaka, Japan, 1988–94), which conjoins technology with an organic use of curving forms. Welsh cites a precedent for such expressive structural deployment in the mid-century work of Eero Saarinen, for example, in his design for the TWA Terminal Building at John F Kennedy Airport (New York, 1956–62), and numerous other examples can be identified within

modernism.[1] Writer and critic Charles Jencks has coined the term 'Organitech' (an expressive variation on the High-Tech theme) to indicate the interpretation of nature and structure in current hybrid approaches.[2] Such a definition might encompass the recent work of Frank Gehry, whose buildings push the envelope of engineering yet remain quintessentially sculptural.

An escalated urge toward the organic and the expressive is just one discernible direction that many contemporary architects take when considering the meaning and purpose of technology in their work. In recent years, the debate has also revolved around the growing presence of the digital as the foremost technological mode and its ramifications in architecture. In a special issue of the magazine *ANY* subtitled 'Mech in tecture', a group of young American architects, theorists and historians grapple with the implications of the machine, the mechanical and technology in architecture at the end of the twentieth century.[3] Collectively, they suggest the difficulty of defining these concepts rigidly in relation to contemporary theory and practice and conclude that machine systems need not be reductive or deterministic but open-ended, as points of departure for architecture. Indeed, this quality of open-endedness informs the work of many younger and mid-career architects whose theory and practice revolves around a technologically inspired architecture that resonates with a machine sensibility.

The work of four architectural practices – Jones, Partners: Architecture, RoT<u>o</u>, Smith-Miller + Hawkinson and TEN Arquitectos – exemplifies individual approaches to the forms, imagery and materials of technology. Rather than celebrating technology for its own sake, however (as in High

1.00 River Rouge Plant
The architecture of heavy
industry is exemplified in Kahn's
design for the Ford plant,
a building shaped by its
responsiveness to servicing
the processes and products
of the Machine Age.

Tech), these architects regard it as fraught with cultural meaning. Their
belief in technology has merged with architectural preoccupations to
provoke a range of more expansive developments, applications and ideas.
The purpose of this book, therefore, is not to identify a specific movement
among architects whose work and ideas differ so widely but to propose a
universal embrace of the technological as a carrier of cultural meaning.
Their range of attitudes toward the use of technological forms, images
and materials convey a responsiveness to the unique and shifting conditions
of late-twentieth-century culture and society.

Historical Antecedents

Modernism's infatuation with technology has permeated architecture in the
twentieth century. In the early modern movement – epitomized in the work
of Auguste Perret, Peter Behrens, Antonio Sant'Elia, Walter Gropius, Erich
Mendelsohn and Le Corbusier – a variety of approaches to technology and
the machine can be discerned. From the exhilarating, vertiginous structures
envisioned by the Italian futurists and the Russian avant-garde to the coolly
rational buildings of the Bauhaus, these European pioneers sought to
incorporate industrial construction techniques and materials alongside
the imagery of manufacturing to make a socially inspired architecture for
a new age, liberated from the constraints and conventions of the past. For
inspiration they often looked to the forms and images of engineering and
the industrial vernacular – grain silos, towers, ships, automobiles – which
for the most part were products of America. The European architects'
lionization of American technical prowess in the 1910s and 1920s, ranging

1.00 Eames House
Adopting an intuitive approach to the combination of off-the-shelf materials in the design and construction of their landmark home and studio, Charles and Ray Eames pioneered an improvisational attitude toward technology that has been highly influential to later generations of architects.

from skyscraper construction to the assembly line, set the stage for their wholehearted acceptance of it.

Less defined by an oppositional relationship to the weight of tradition, American architects of the same period often masked their technological innovation in conventional forms, as in the case of such early landmark skyscrapers as Cass Gilbert's Woolworth Building (New York City, 1913) and Raymond Hood's Chicago Tribune Tower (1923–25). Not until the late 1920s and 1930s, as the 'Machine Age' sensibility emerged, could technology as a powerfully seductive image of optimism and confidence be discerned as a widespread characteristic in American architecture. This resulted in part from European influence and legitimization, as the machine-oriented work and ideas of such architects as Le Corbusier became known in architectural circles. With affinities to the International Style's emphasis on rigorous simplicity, efficiency and lack of ornamentation, the Machine Age allowed architects to see buildings as machines and to endow them with an aura of science and industry.[4]

Dynamic, streamlined forms loomed large during the interwar period, echoing the curvature of mechanized elements and implying speed and industrial precision. In a time dominated by a machine aesthetic, the factory became an increasingly iconic and formidable frame of reference. A large number of works in the 1920s and 1930s, including Albert Kahn's River Rouge Plant for Ford Motor Company (Michigan, 1917–39) and Buckminster Fuller's design for an industrially assembled 'Dymaxion (dynamic plus maximum efficiency) House', manifested an enthusiastic embrace of the machine and its possibilities for giving form to new ways of living, working

and consuming in the twentieth century. Revealing an infatuation with this new potential, a 'machine-made' future captured the imagination of the architectural vanguard and the American public. Introducing a technological aesthetic in their work on a range of building types that included many of the great bridges, dams and power stations built under the aegis of the WPA (Works Projects Administration) and the TVA (Tennessee Valley Authority) in the 1930s, numerous architects exalted in the imagery of the machine as an embodiment of American strength and achievement.

Following the technological advances developed during the Second World War, as mass-manufacturing hastened a new consumerism in American society, an increasingly refined industrial sensibility continued to develop in modern architecture that further underscored the idea and image of factory production. Progress in engineering gave rise to an emphasis on structure, making possible the attainment of ever-greater heights in skyscrapers and a body of remarkable structural experiments in the 1950s and 1960s using such materials as concrete by architects around the world ranging from Le Corbusier, Eero Saarinen and Paul Rudolph to Félix Candela and Oscar Niemeyer.

Maison de Verre and the Eames House

Two works of residential architecture conceived in the first half of the twentieth century were pivotal in the later developments in the use of technology in architecture. The first example, Pierre Chareau's Maison de Verre (Glass House, Paris, 1928–32), was the transformation of a small building in an urban courtyard into a house and doctor's office by means of

1.00 Maison de Verre
An ingenious solution to inserting new architecture within a dense, historical urban setting, the Maison de Verre as viewed from the street is rigorously machined. However, its presence and relationship to the buildings that surround it is softened by the textured luminosity of its predominantly glass-brick façade.

ingenious planning and the application of industrial materials and techniques. Structurally, the design is audacious in that the main part of the building is deftly inserted into a framework of exposed steel supports and constitutes the first level of a three-level design; the two upper floors of the residence are clad in glass brick to allow light to reach the lower levels. Other noteworthy devices, used for the first time in a domestic context, are visible energy conduits, mechanical ventilation shutters and industrial handrails that double as bookshelves – all mechanisms that are revealed and displayed. Throughout Chareau's design an innovative technological aesthetic is evident, which has not only been a critical source of inspiration to practitioners of High Tech but an antecedent for a broader spectrum of technology-based work in its myriad unconventional possibilities for combination.

An even stronger forerunner of the sensibility that now animates much contemporary work, the Charles and Ray Eames house and studio was designed and built between 1945 and 1949 in the Pacific Palisades area of Los Angeles. A startlingly unique admixture of standardized prefabricated industrial components and highly intuitive combinatorial processes thanks to its modular construction system, the house is consummately experimental not only in the use of industrial materials and imagery, but also in terms of the liberties taken with them. Conjoining its parts in an improvisational way, the designers turned elements such as the use of colour, texture and image into significant sections of the building, a bold departure from the rational and machined emphases of their contemporaries.

1.00 House LE
In the kitchen-dining area of
this compact house located in a
dense residential neighbourhood
of Mexico City, the architect
relies on an elegant combination
of such low-cost materials as
glass, metal and wood and on
a sequence of simple sectioned
layers to enhance and to amplify
the compact plan and to create
partially screened and private
yet flowing spaces.

By tracing its reception among younger architects including Peter
Smithson, Richard Rogers and Renzo Piano in Europe and Craig Ellwood in
California, historian Reyner Banham refers to the Eames House as the genesis
of postwar High Tech.[5] Banham argues that despite its intended origin as
a prototype, the Eames House can also be regarded as the forerunner of a
more recent attitude about technology in architecture that is experimental,
intuitive and improvisational – characteristics that are generally foreign to
conventional High-Tech vocabulary. To this end, Banham cites a 1966 article
by Michael Brawne entitled 'The Wit of Technology', in which the author
comments, 'Where the Eames House differs, however, from its nearest
predecessors . . . is that its composition is wholly additive, with frame and
cladding not separated, but working together, and that it possesses wit, a
quality extremely rare in architecture. Its wit is, of course, largely the result
of the additive process, of the seemingly casual juxtaposition of different
elements.'[6] For architects today, the crucial lessons of the Eames House are
the privileging of the ad hoc and the modular gesture and the designers'
alacrity in profoundly rethinking how industrial, off-the-shelf building
components can be applied in a residential context. Furthermore, the
Eameses' reinterpretation of the prototype signifies as much about the
freedom and possibility at a crucial historical moment in a particular
geographical and cultural context as it does about their personal
predilections and inventiveness as designers.

　　　　The architects whose work is presented here are profiled in terms
of the way their buildings manifest an experimentalism with technology.
From a variety of viewpoints and positions, these architects approach

1.00 Brill Residence
The remodel of the two-storey main space shows the defining presence of steel – complete with pulleys, gantrys, cables and other mechanistic components not customarily applied in a residential interior – as the framework for interior divisions.

technology and the machine as an established expression of cultural meaning that is particular to a time and historical circumstance. Their response to these conditions has, in turn, reshaped and redefined the presence of technology in buildings that we use every day.

In a vastly different historical and ideological moment from that of the mid-century, today's architectural culture permits and perhaps demands an expanded, inclusive sensibility shaped by the paradoxes of our own age, one that feeds upon past and present. At the end of the twentieth century, the machine can no longer be considered as the promise of the future in broad cultural terms: it is already an inescapable presence. We have entered an era in which the meaning and symbolism of technology is continuously reinterpreted and reassessed, and its potential seems to alternately inspire and perplex. The implications for architecture are significant. Whereas advances in technology and the machine have clearly had an impact on architecture, obvious technological engagement is only one of many communication devices available to architects.
In a time of pluralism, use of such imagery is a deliberate decision to reinterpret and connect with its unavoidable presence rather than be a product of its development. For architects who adopt expanded references to the machine beyond the realm of High Tech, technology stands as a primarily cultural preoccupation signifying a variety of histories, conditions and meanings that infuse architecture with an almost narrative content and substance.

The selection of work – its exuberant, dynamic and frank signification for Wes Jones, its theoretical and material implications for Henry Smith-

1.00 Maison de Verre
With a double-height window-wall surface articulated in glass block, the space within the Maison de Verre also houses a variety of industrial components and technological products that had not previously been used in a domestic context.

Miller and Laurie Hawkinson, its embodiment of urbanity and internationalism in Enrique Norten at TEN Arquitectos and its improvisational imperative for Michael Rotondi and Clark Stevens at RoT<u>o</u> – reveals a plethora of attitudes and possibilities toward the use of technology as an architectural language inseparable from the framework of contemporary culture.

Notes

1   John Welsh, 'On a Wing and a Layer – Technorganic is the 1990s', *RIBA Journal* (July 1994), pp 22–29

2   Charles Jencks, 'High-Tech Slides to Organi-tech', *ANY* (Architecture New York, no 10, 1995), pp 44–49

3   Wes Jones (guest ed.), 'Mech in 'tecture: Reconsidering Materialism in the Electronic Era', *ANY* (Architecture New York, no 10, 1995)

4   Richard Guy Wilson, Dianne Pilgrim, and Dickran Tashjian, *The Machine Age in America* (New York: The Brooklyn Museum in association with Harry N. Abrams, Inc., 1986)

5   Reyner Banham, 'Klarheit, Ehrlichkeit, Einfachkeit . . . and *Wit* Too!: The Case Study Houses in the World's Eyes', *Blueprints for Modern Living: History and Legacy of the Case Study Houses* (Cambridge [MA] and London: The MIT Press, 1989), pp 183–95

6   Michael Brawne, 'The Wit of Technology', *Architectural Design* (September 1966), pp 449–57

1.11

1.12

1.13

1.14

Jones, Partners: Architecture
"Dynamo"

The work of Jones, Partners: Architecture (J,P:A) reveals an almost romantic fascination with the machine as a key signifier and carrier of meaning, and has been acclaimed for its 'critical manipulations of technology'. Often projecting and evoking the forms of machines, or incorporating such mechanical devices as gantries, actuators, complex transformational linkages or hydraulic systems, J,P:A's work shares the spirit of the avant-garde Russian architect Iakov Chernikov, whose strikingly graphic drawings of buildings as machines appeared in the 1931 treatise *The Construction of Architectural and Machine Forms*. As in Chernikov's visionary drawings of unbuilt turbine-like works, J,P:A's buildings are fully integrated designs with all their composite parts operating in harmony.

Founding partner Wes Jones's profound interest in technology permeated his early work as design principal and partner in Holt Hinshaw Pfau Jones, for example, the Astronaut's Memorial at the Kennedy Space Center (Florida, 1987–89) and Paramount Film and Tape Archives (Los Angeles, 1989–90). It is also apparent in his work at J,P:A in the UCLA Chiller Plant Facilities Complex (Los Angeles, 1990–94, p 28) and in the Confluence Point Bridges and Ranger Station (San Jose, California,

1992–97, p 29). His use of industrial materials, forms and mechanisms imparts a raw, energetic power from the structures' real, latent and implied dynamism. That some of these buildings frankly incorporate working mechanical elements is a particular feature of the work.

Jones's commitment to the machine is captured in his writings and lectures, many of which have been collected in *Instrumental Form: Designs for Words, Buildings, Machines*[1], where a diagrammatic graphic language accentuates the buildings' character. In stark contrast to the more refined approach of orthodox European High Tech – or, as he terms it, 'haute tech' – Jones's evocation of the machine is a particularly American portrayal, viewing it as a tool rather than an ideal. Architectural form that incorporates the machine is evidence of a culture that exhibits irrepressible exuberance, frankness and purpose.

The robust nature of the practice's recent work reveals a buoyant, experimental approach, less concerned with imagery than with function. In their use of technology as an operational language, Jones's designs emphatically contradict the reductive nature of functionalism. He described his approach in a recent lecture, 'We tease technology into unhiddenness through expressive excess, through an interest in expression beyond efficiency'.[2] Embracing the visible, honest, workmanlike aspect of technology, his work proves how architecture at a variety of scales – from furniture to urban design – not only emphasizes technology's function and revels in how it operates, but shows how each design solves a set of 'mechanical' challenges posed by its programme and function. Jones's ideas parallel the concept of *techne* – the process of creation that is guided by the thing made, by its own will rather than the maker's; a way of revealing that is honest to the object's will-to-form. In today's architectural climate, this is not an uncontroversial position, so it is only natural that J,P:A's work contains components of irony and humour.

Dedicated to producing a sense of the remarkable in our environment, J,P:A fosters the pragmatic and poetic potential of technology in architecture in a search for a machine-like anonymity. 'Such a practice eschews a personality-based formalism,' he writes. 'We prefer to stand behind the object, rather than in front of it. Viewers are encouraged to engage the work directly and become the authors of their own reading. This engagement is marked by a distinctly modern sense of optimism, tempered by the realization that confidence can never be taken for granted . . . . An appreciation of the legibility of mechanical reference – a sense of its appropriateness as a frame for the contemporary condition – gives form to these attitudes. The aim of such an architecture is to capture the feeling of the contemporary, the expression of a *now* which will someday become *then* gracefully, in a future that is neither anxious or complacent.'[3]

Notes

1   Wes Jones, *Instrumental Form: Designs for Words, Buildings, Machines* (New York: Princeton University Press, 1998)

2   Notes for a lecture given by Wes Jones in 1998

3   Statement from Jones, Partners: Architecture's firm profile

UCLA Chiller Plant Facilities Complex
Los Angeles, 1990–94

1.1

The main power plant at UCLA and the shops and offices of the campus's facilities-maintenance department are organized to make visible the technological extremes necessary to offer comfort in the desert climate of Los Angeles. The building's components are articulated according to programme, yet they highlight and critique the conventional attitude that takes technology for granted without acknowledging the reality of its efforts. Providing power and chilled water for current and forecast campus needs, the Chiller Plant features turbine-driven centrifugal and absorption chillers, pumps, water demineralization equipment and electrical distribution systems. While sensitive to its surroundings, the building makes no attempt to conceal its plant machinery, proudly displaying the inherently engaging qualities of technology as an integrated and carefully considered part of the structural composition. While the use of familiar materials and architectural treatments is critical in application, rather than imitative, the façade's screens, typically used to conceal equipment, are thus revealed as masks. Furthermore, since the client and context for the plant is an educational institution, it seems appropriate to underscore the building's typology and make a didactic display of its screening apparatus.

Confluence Point Bridges and Ranger Station
San Jose, California, 1992–97

1.12 This information centre for an urban park was created as part of a US Army Corps of Engineers flood-control project. The initial programme, including concrete channels, rip-rap (medium-sized stones set into concrete for erosion control) and widening of the river, was expanded into a significant urban amenity: the Guadalupe River Park. Developed as a unique civic feature, the site and its bridges provide a critical link between downtown San Jose and its new sports arena. In a considered response to the context and programme and in its unselfconscious forms and details, the building is conceived as a piece of equipment to be used. Sincere and straightforward application of honest materials, such as concrete, cement plaster, a weathering steel structural frame and metal siding, enhances the architecture's robustness. The project consists of a single structure that mediates between tower, man-made and located at the street's edge, and nature. Similar to the UCLA Chiller Plant, the design acknowledges the structure's function for flood control while underscoring the relationship of the building to the natural forces it is designed to mitigate. The architectural forms evoke the artificial character of the park in the new 'river' channel, which will remain when the structure's origins are forgotten.

The Golden Plate, Union Square
San Francisco, 1997

1.13

In an urban renewal project in downtown San Francisco, J,P:A redesigned an existing landmark urban square atop a civic car park for security, aesthetic and mercantile reasons. The outcome was a machine, covering an entire city block and dubbed 'The Golden Plate'. Resting on massive steel trusses, the 'park' is essentially composed of two large metal plates inclined upward into the air to ensure views across the site and to reveal the formerly hidden car park. The effect of the tilting is to reduce car-park crime, to allow light and ventilation into the subterranean structure and to suggest a critique of the park's current function. Each plate supports one or more of the park's disparate activities, conceived with an honesty of purpose akin to that of the other great San Francisco infrastructural landmark, the Golden Gate Bridge: one plate bears a stage for outdoor performance, the other has seating and a lawn. Entering from the street or from the parking below, visitors ascend long narrow ramps that emphasize the dynamic, animating quality of circulation. While the model for this unbuilt project has been described as resembling military machines – stealth bombers and aircraft carriers – J,P:A extends the notion of the machine to a larger, urban context.

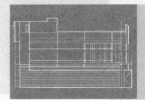

1.14

Brill Residence
Silverlake, California, 1998–99

A new steel structural system inserted into the shell of an existing 2,500-square-foot (233-square-metre) martial-arts studio yields a spacious hillside residence for a jazz drummer and his son. The floor that separated the work-out area from the garage level was removed to create a three-storey living space in half of the resulting volume, and a stacked tier of private spaces in the other half. The living area features display shelving an extensive drum collection, accessed by a mechanical crane bridge with safety rails that allow it to double as a performance platform. Opaque and translucent wall panels on a sliding rail system ensure privacy in the loft-style residence and can also be used to optimize the space's acoustics. Striving neither to showcase a High-Tech idiom nor to reject it, the project casts a technological eye upon the opportunities and constraints of an extant residential programme. The systematic spatial reorganization is clear – the proliferation of sliding panels for versatility, the travelling crane bridge as a direct solution to the problem of access and the overall effect of the new steel framing as a confident expression of the infrastructure – all reveal precisely the function they serve.

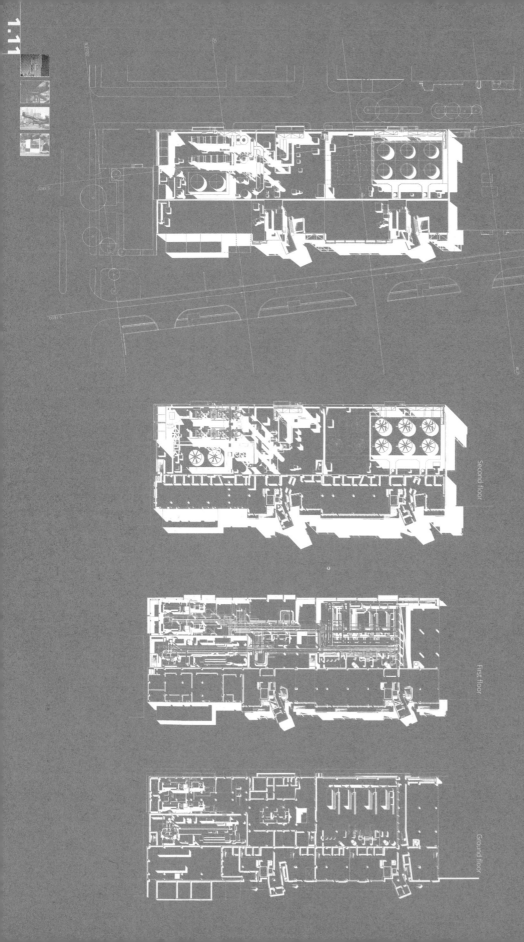

Site plan

Second floor

First floor

Ground floor

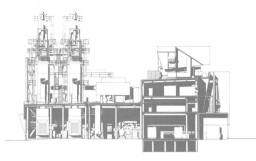

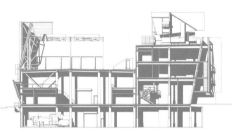

Cross sections

1.11 UCLA Chiller Plant

Instead of concealing its primary function as a power plant, the almost exaggerated industrial appearance of this building draws attention to and even dramatizes its infrastructural role. In a centrally located and quite dense sector of the UCLA campus, it houses a number of water- and electricity-related functions, as well as workshops and offices for campus facilities maintenance.

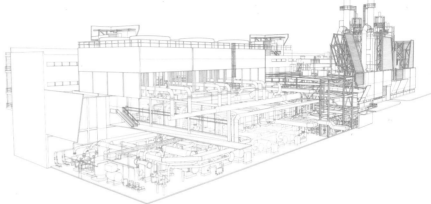

View from southwest

1.11 UCLA Chiller Plant
Designed for a phased
construction on a tight site, the
workshops and offices of the
facility are positioned around
the building's interior while the
power plant occupies the
streetfront, which is only
partially masked by brick veneer
and metal panels.

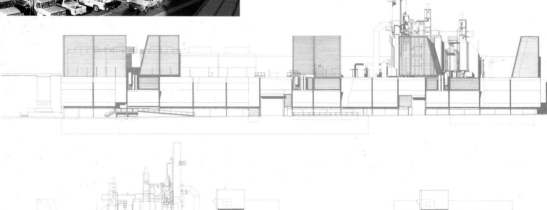

South elevation

North elevation

1.12 Confluence Point
Conjoining a series of stairs and
ramps with a tower-like main space,
the building uses these elements in
a dynamic configuration to invite
visitors' active exploration of the
structure and to underscore its
relationship to a geographical
point of confluence: two rivers
within a park

Site plan

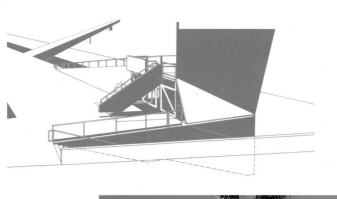

1.12 Confluence Point
The project consists of three simple structures: a short truss bridge constructed of pre-manufactured weathering steel elements, a 'log' bridge of post-tensioned concrete and a building in which both elements are combined.

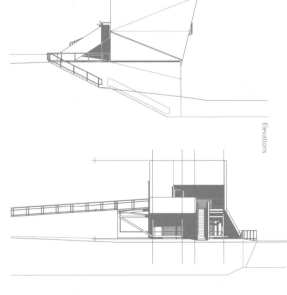

Elevations

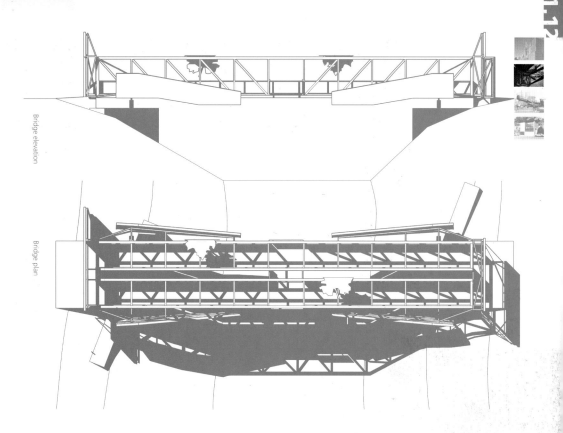

Bridge elevation

Bridge plan

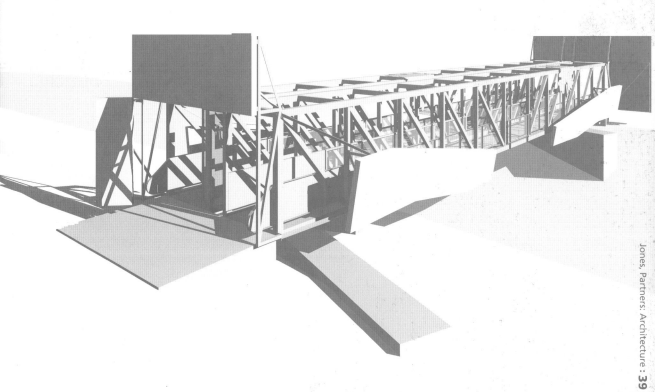

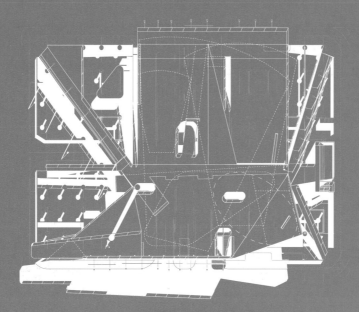

Site plan

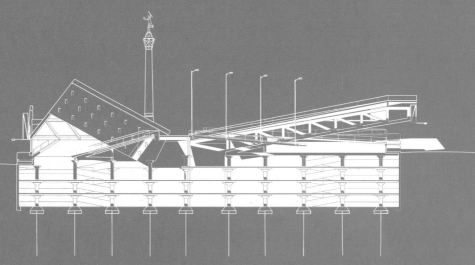

Section

1.13 The Golden Plate
Aiming to generate and expose
activity on multiple levels –
below ground, at grade and
above ground – the project's
layout also allows for points of
interchange at the connections
between these zones. Above
ground, the two intersecting
plates lift into the air to provide
such urban amenities as a stage
for outdoor performance,
seating and a grassy lawn, while
underground parking is partially
revealed by the lifting plates.

1.14 Brill Residence

While maintaining the basic footprint of the existing building, J.P.A's residential remodel extends and reworks its already quasi-industrial vocabulary into an emphatic one. Devising an experimental system of interior spatial dividers within a steel framework allows the double-height main living area to become an active and potentially flexible space.

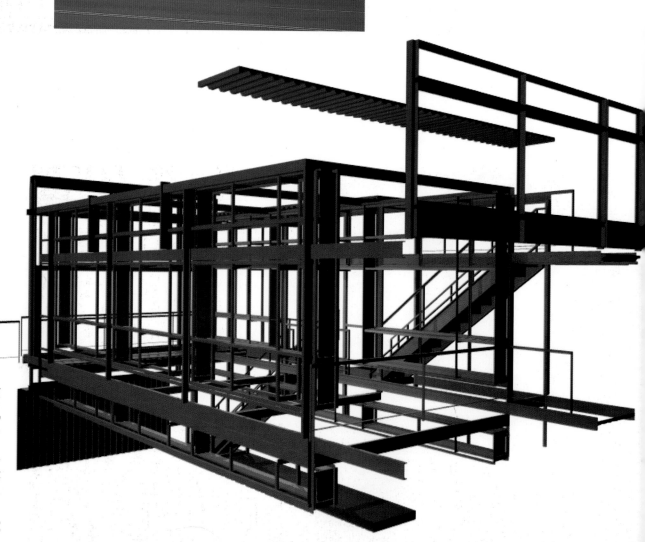

Elevations

Sections

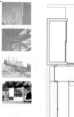

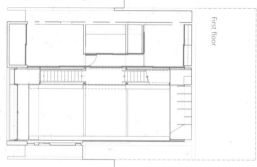

First floor

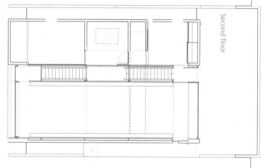

Second floor

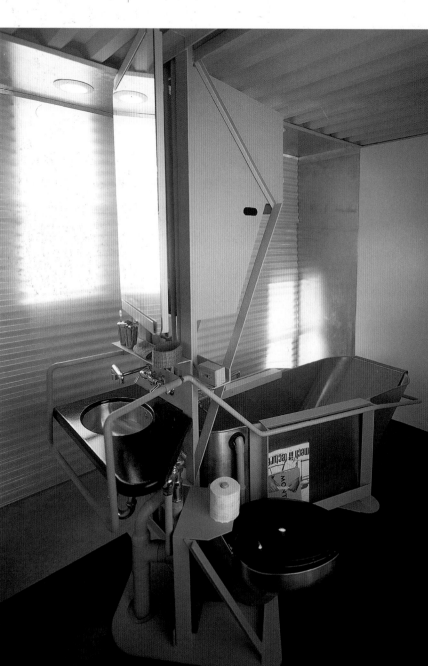

1.14 Brill Residence
The industrial feel is carried through to the freestanding, multifunction bathroom unit, an ingenious exercise in utility. In the central double-height space, the geometry and dynamism of the steel-frame structure is multiplied by the play of light and shadow.

1.21

1.22

1.23

1.24

TEN Arquitectos
Machine as Invention and Critique

1.20 The work of Enrique Norten and his practice, TEN Arquitectos, consciously uses the imagery and materials of the machine to express a globalized, late twentieth-century sensibility in architecture. In many respects, their approach is a polemic reaction to the work of a previous generation when Mexican identity was articulated in terms of monumentality and folkloric references, epitomized in the work of Luis Barragán, Pedro Ramirez Vasquez, Tepdoro Gonzales de Leon and Ricardo Legorreta. In contrast, motivated by internationalism, TEN Arquitectos pursues inventive, overtly technological strategies to reveal an interest in the legacy of constructivism within the modern movement. However, TEN's persistent use of an industrial vocabulary is partly derived from a responsiveness to the conditions of modern Mexican life and highlights a politics of culture by means of its subtle contextualism.

Norten and his partner, Bernardo Gómez-Pimienta, compose their buildings with a diversity of technologically derived materials, including metal, glass and suspension systems. Frequent use of metal for roofs and façades evokes the simple industrial sheds common to Mexico, but also emphasizes transparency, dynamism, buoyancy and structural tension when incorporated in their designs. Their work also offers startlingly complex, layered spatial sequences that depart strongly from the sense of enclosure and the archaeological tendency previously seen as hallmarks of Mexican architecture. Embodying the energy of urbanity, particularly that of the chaotic and transitional character that animates Mexico City, Norten's architecture has been described as 'precision-made and technologically innovative, hospitable to the speed and flexibility of modernity.'[1] As Michael Sorkin has noted, 'in Mexico, modernist forms retain the aura of progress . . . TEN's work, in its Mexican-ness, is strongly associated with an architectural tradition that is still unfolding, a modernism still directly

connected to its origins rather than – as with so much practice today – simply conducting a reappropriation of images that have long outlived their original vitality.'[2]

TEN Arquitectos was founded by Enrique Norten in 1985 and his partner, Bernardo Gómez-Pimienta, joined the firm in 1987. The practice has worked on many different types of projects, including residential, commercial, cultural and educational centres, furniture design, single-family apartments and houses and park and urban redevelopments. Noteworthy projects include Workers' Housing for the Program of Urban Saturation of INFONAVIT at the Historic Center of Mexico City (1992), Televisa Multipurpose Hall (San Angel, Mexico City, 1993), the National School of Theater (Churubusco, Mexico City, 1993–94, p 52), renovation of Insurgentes Theater (Mexico City, 1995), Televisa Mixed-Use Building (Mexico City, 1993–95, p 53), the Museum of Natural History (Chapultepec, Mexico City, 1995), the Camino Real Heritage Community Center and Museum (Saucer, New Mexico, 1997), the Adams Hall Gallery and School of Fine Arts at the University of Pennsylvania (Philadelphia, 1997) and additions to and renovation of the College of Art and Architecture at the University of Michigan (Ann Arbor, 1997).

The work of TEN Arquitectos is known for its contemporary motivation, uniting the aspirations of the modern world with the traditions of their native Mexican culture and environment. Their work has won awards in the Buenos Aires Biennial (1993), the Mexican Biennials (1990, 1992, 1994, 1996), and the first Iberoamerican Biennial of Architecture and Engineering in Madrid (1998). Their Televisa Mixed-Use Building in Mexico City was termed the 'best Latin American building of the decade' by the Mies van der Rohe Foundation in Barcelona.

Notes

1   Richard Ingersoll, Terence Riley and Michael Sorkin, *TEN Arquitectos: Enrique Norten – Bernardo Gómez-Pimienta* (New York, The Monacelli Press, 1998), p 31
2   Michael Sorkin, *op. cit.*, p 15

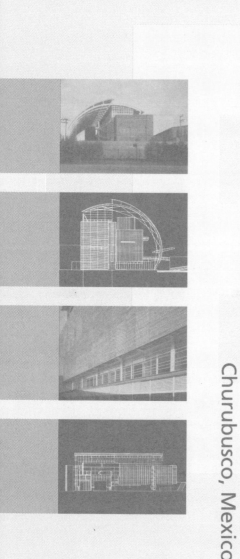

National School of Theater, National Center for the Arts

Churubusco, Mexico City, 1993–94

1.21 A steel-sheathed hangar-like structure with a vertiginous pattern of circulation, the National School of Theater embodies the dynamism of the machine, not only as a response to its complex programme but as a reflection of its site adjacent to the meeting of two heavily trafficked, major freeways. Its arching shell resembles the industrial warehouse sheds common to such urban peripheries. The striking curvature, gleaming surface and the building's sheer size compound its status as an urban icon and marker for the rest of the campus. The shell encloses an assemblage of volumes, each one a tectonic expression of a different use. In material and dimension, the spaces have unique textures, tones and personalities; for example, a ship-shaped library is veneered in tropical hardwood and a three-storey box screened by redwood slats disguises the southern façade. The box contains a rehearsal space and classrooms and serves as the architectural antithesis of the glinting carapace on the exterior. Organized in a seemingly ad hoc manner, these volumes are in fact arranged logically in terms of circulation and their respective function within the cavernous, continuous shell, which acts as a unifying backdrop. The main space is completely open at both ends like a tunnel, providing a meeting place not only for the building's visitors and costumes but for the opposing forces of chaos and order found within the building.

Televisa Mixed-Use Building
Mexico City, 1993–95

1.22 Like the National School of Theater, Norten's mixed-use building for Televisa in Mexico City projects a highly machined appearance, but one that is decidedly different in character. Of seemingly greater solidity and mass, the Televisa building incorporates a sophisticated array of materials and technologies, resulting in a sleek and well-crafted appearance that reflects the higher budget of its corporate client. In both cases, however, the two major components of the structures are the roof and façade – curving forms that signal motion, fluidity and interaction within a dynamic urban context.

Immersed in the complexity of downtown Mexico City, a trapezoidal lot comprises the building's site – a solitary, unique floating island of space anchored in the chaotic urban setting. The client was searching for a new image for the company as an urban icon and requested various functions be integrated in a single building. This union of distinct and independent needs resulted in two superimposed forms. Addressing the scale of the city, the public parking facility conforms to the street's urban space, where social activities are defined by a silvery, elliptical shell. The shell curves in on itself, exposing a hard exoskeleton to the main vehicular artery. In contrast, the service floor creates a transparent, formless transition between the two forms and a series of vertical and horizontal circulation cores connect the overlaid forms. Two interior ramps access the primary dining facility and serve as a street-level billboard, establishing an architectural vocabulary through the use of visual media and by assuming the structural and spatial roles of a wall.

House LE
Mexico City, 1994–95

1.23 TEN Arquitectos approached the urban residential lot by dividing it longitudinally rather than transversely. The result is a long narrow building, essentially one room wide. Rational in arrangement as in construction, it reflects the site's compact nature, the limited budget and the family's simple needs. The house has layers of slender sections that run its entire length, perpendicular to the street and that are subtly transcribed on to the otherwise modest façade. L-shaped in plan, the design positions service quarters and a garage in the short wing, while allowing the long axis to remain a continuous space opening on to a split-level patio with a screened southern exposure. The open-plan layout enables the living room to flow around a kitchen space that forms a translucent box. Layers and transitions are accomplished through the use of zones of glass, louvres of redwood and patios that maintain a relationship to the exterior. House LE is not such an obvious technological statement as some of TEN's other buildings. The house's fundamental make-up comprises walls of exposed concrete and concrete block with plaster, within an exposed steel structure. The bedrooms, on the second level, have redwood slats hanging from the eaves to shield large expanses of sliding plate glass. Closed to the street and completely open and transparent inside, the house fulfils the family's desire to enjoy the intensity and energy of the city, while maintaining privacy and intimacy.

JVC Exhibition and Convention Center

Guadalajara, Mexico, 1998–onward

1.24 This project forms part of the JVC Cultural and Business Center, a complex of buildings that will also include a commercial centre, a museum, a cinema, a hotel, housing, a fairground and a theatre, each to be designed by a different architect. The site is close to a nature reserve with excellent views. TEN's design for the centre consists of a main building, three secondary volumes and a flexible space intended for exterior exhibitions, all located on a large plaza beside an artificial lake. The main, oval-shaped building will be covered with a very light translucent membrane. In order to conserve energy, the membrane will allow the passage of natural light into the interior during the day, whereas at night, the building will resemble a huge lamp visible from Guadalajara. In this manner it will become a landmark, not only because of its size but also due to its changing appearance from night to day. The building will have no columns: it will be based on a steel structure conforming to a grid that follows an oval form. The plan shows that its functional areas are laid out in a series of concentric rings, with a central space for exhibitions. The first ring comprises support areas for the centre, surrounded by a revolving ramp to allow visitors to pass through and to view the different levels. The outermost rings contain lobbies and an exterior loading ramp.

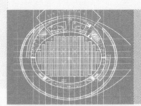

1.21

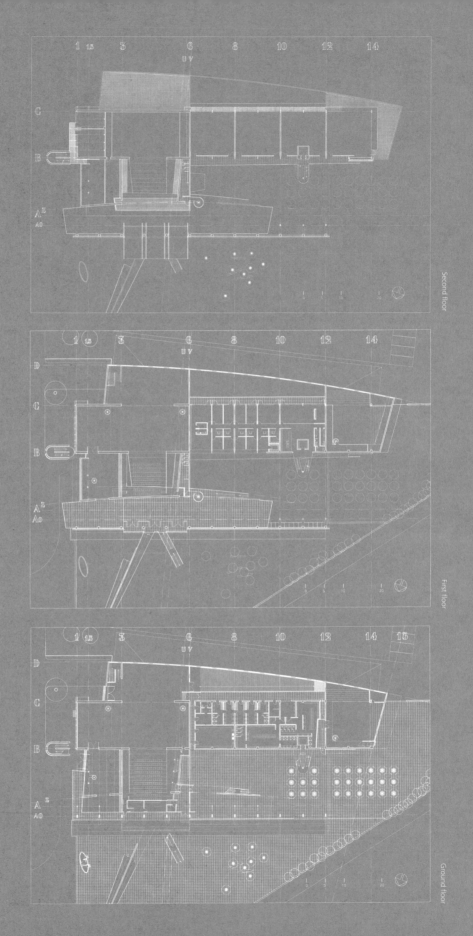

Second floor

First floor

Ground floor

1.21 National School of Theater

Subtly evoking yet profoundly rethinking the Mexican tradition of monumental public spaces, the vast open lobby is shaped by the sweeping curve of the roof that mediates between sun and shade, wet and dry, the urban scale of the exterior and the intimacy of the interior landscape that it shelters. Seemingly held in place by taut tie rods, the coiled steel pipes appear to be straining under great pressure, but only support a lightweight corrugated-steel roof.

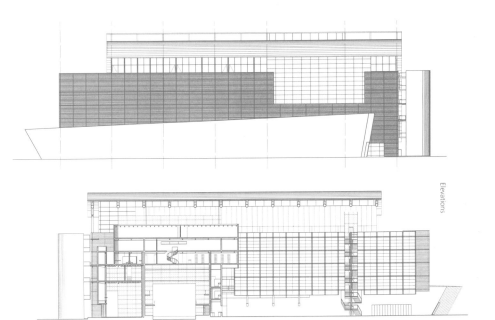

Elevations

TEN Arquitectos : **57**

1.21 National School of Theater

While physically protecting the inner pavilions from the elements, the open enclosure also defines and organizes a series of heterogeneous volumes containing classrooms, theatres, and service spaces. Industrial materials used throughout, such as corrugated metal and concrete, reflect not only the international architectural vocabulary of modernism but also their importance in Mexican vernacular usage.

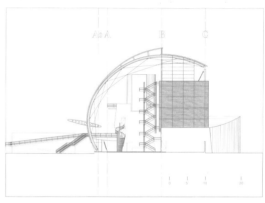

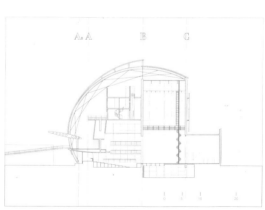

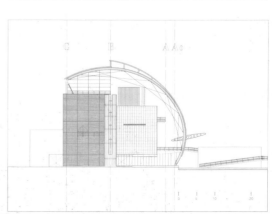

Cross sections

1.22 Televisa Mixed-Use Building

A sleek technological fortress for a corporate client, this visually transparent space hovers above a blank, masonry barricade of hand-polished black concrete, cocooned beneath a monumental glass-and-steel bubble. Simultaneously roof and façade, the metallic, elliptical shell is the building's foremost feature. Also important is the large glass curtain wall: its surface appears as a beacon when seen from the city and, from the inside, as a picture screen displaying the city beyond. Its supports are rigorously delineated – every cable, spar and joint elegantly revealed and expressed.

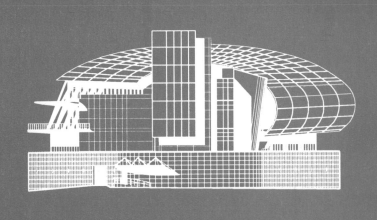

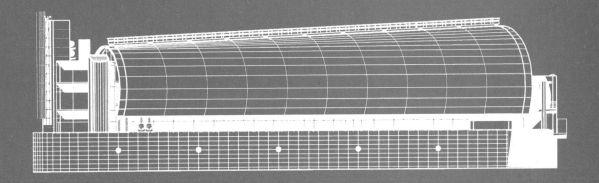

Elevations

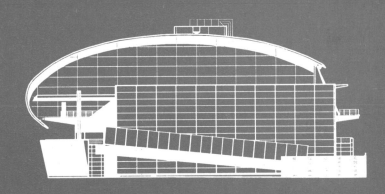

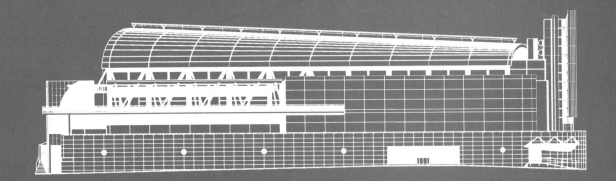

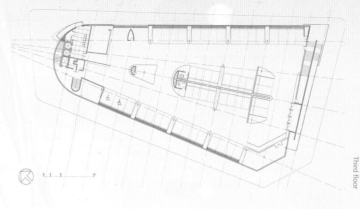

Third floor

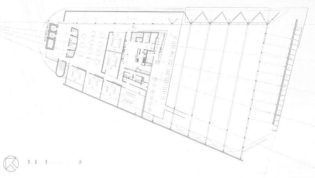

Second floor

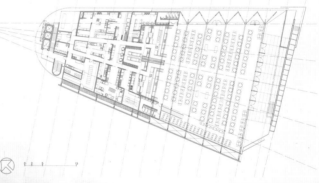

Ground floor

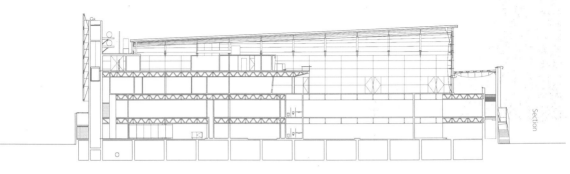

Section

1.22 Televisa Mixed-Use Building
Interplay between the shell's structure and its interior cladding allows ambiguity to creep into the composition. A smooth, unmarked, diaphanous skin shrouds joints where one would expect to see a clear expression of structural connections. Tie rods float in space and pipe columns puncture the floor and ceiling, negating the perception of any tangible sensation of tension or compression.

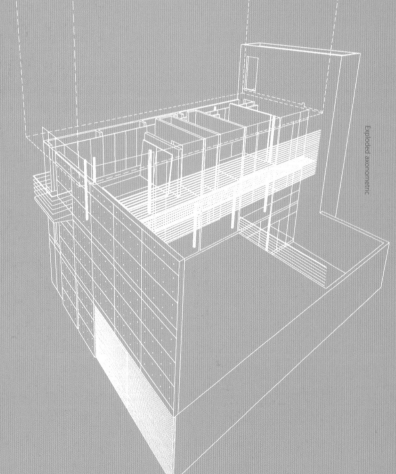

Exploded axonometric

1.23 House LE
Rotated ninety degrees away from the street, this compact house in a dense residential neighbourhood is organized to allow all rooms to face a long courtyard that runs the length of the property. Establishing an artificial ground plane, its private courtyard is raised one storey above street level to accommodate the service spaces below. Interior detailing includes poured concrete walls, polished wood floors and sliding glass walls separated from the exposed structure of round steel-pipe columns. The cantilevered open steel grate that extends across the length of the bedrooms on one level of the house, is surrounded by a full-height guardrail of horizontal redwood slats.

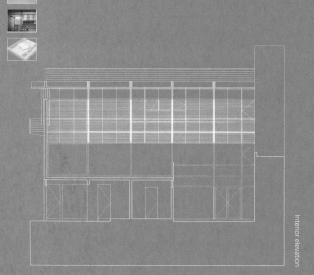

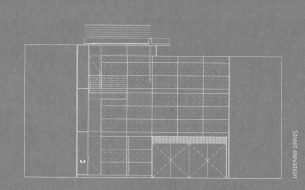

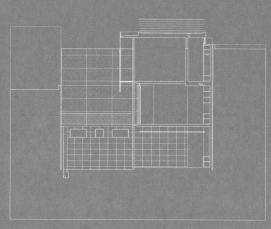

Interior elevation

Street elevation

Sections

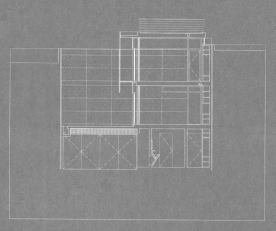

1.23 House LE
Inward-looking to ensure privacy, the house presents a closed, carefully detailed and scaled street wall to the exterior. All windows facing the street are either high clerestory windows or made from translucent glass and no openings overlook the street from the sun-filled courtyard.

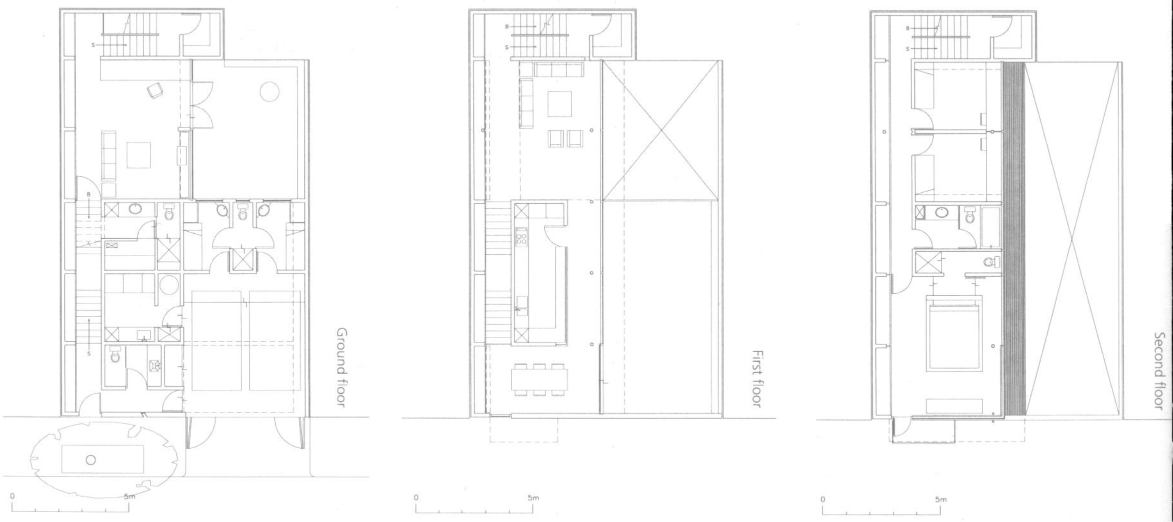

Ground floor

First floor

Second floor

0   5m

0   5m

0   5m

1.23 House LE

The house's spatial zones are arranged in two directions: horizontally, the structure places services on the ground level, public rooms on the first floor and private spaces above; vertical layering is expressed by sandwiching the rooms between an interior passage along the property line and the loggia fronting the courtyard. Zones between the living room and kitchen are formed by a translucent glass wall that creates a narrow passage and dramatically expresses the contemporary ideal of the kitchen as the centre of family life.

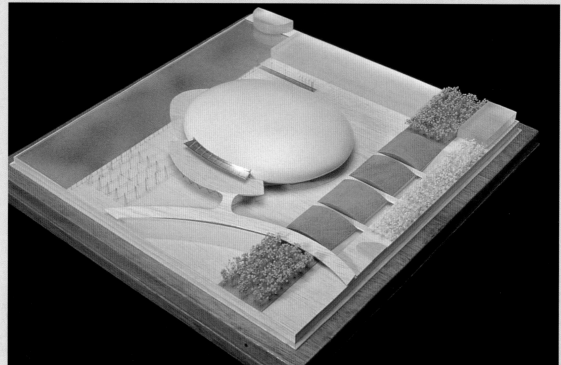

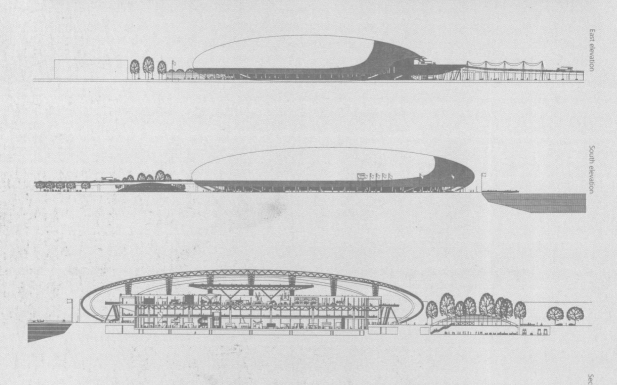

East elevation

South elevation

Sections

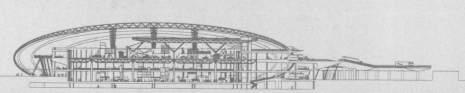

Ground floor

First floor

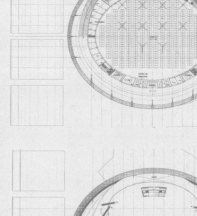

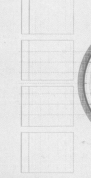

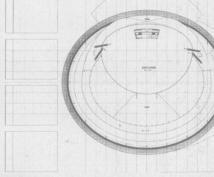

Second floor

Third floor

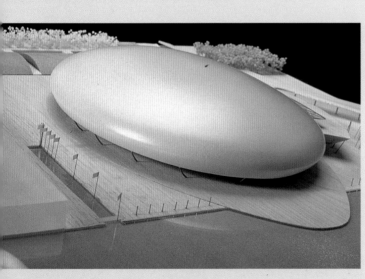

1.24 JVC Center

In this project, now in development, an efficient space-frame structure allows the roof enclosure to span the entire volume of the building. This lightweight structural system, to be clad in uniformly coloured and translucent fabric, will give the centre the appearance of a giant white bubble floating on the waters of the adjacent lake. The exterior vehicular ramp, which allows service vehicles to drive directly on to the exhibition floor, visually tethers the building to the shore.

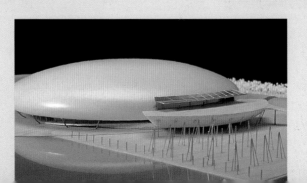

1.30 RoTo

1.31

1.32

1.33

1.34

RoTo
The Industrial and the
Improvisational

1.30 The work of Michael Rotondi and Clark Stevens at RoTo Architects, established in 1991, exemplifies a laconic approach to the machine. While the forms, images and materials of technology appear with some frequency throughout their work, their utilization depends on the unique circumstances and exigencies of each project, site and client. Reflecting a design methodology that is both contextual and improvisational, RoTo has an open-ended, fluid interpretation of the machine as one of many components from which to draw inspiration.

Departing from a literal application of a technological idiom, the idea of machine as organism is perhaps the most salient characteristic of RoTo's work. An intricate accumulation and interrelation of parts defines the design of the Teiger House (New Jersey, 1996), making it appear somewhat transitional from the direction of Rotondi's earlier partnership in the Morphosis studio. The Gemini Consulting Learning Center (New Jersey, 1995), built for the same client (whose profession is business forecasting), demonstrates the practice's ideas about flexibility stemming from concepts of dynamic human organization. The diversity of RoTo's approach is manifest in their work, for

example, Nicola Restaurant (Los Angeles, 1993), Dorland Mountain Arts Colony (Temecula, California, 1994, p 76), Warehouse C Exhibition Hall and Public Gardens (Nagasaki, Japan, 1997, p 78) and Xiyuan Buddhist Monastery School (Suzhou, China, 1997–onward).

As a guiding principle, RoTo believes in a systematic approach and cites R M Schindler as a source of inspiration. Instead of following an earlier generation's wholehearted advocacy of a machine aesthetic, RoTo approaches the machine in terms of the application of logic within each architectural work. Michael Rotondi comments, 'Our projects are not intended to give form to technology: they are meant to give form to life, and technology facilitates our efforts. The expressive nature of the work is an index, a building recording the history of its process of having been made. The basis of our choices, throughout the design process, takes into consideration the absolute precision of our minds and the relative precision of our bodies. The machine mediates. The next consideration is the relationship between high-tech and high-touch; the interdependence of both is essential to our existence.'[1]

The practice has completed a wide range of projects of varying scope and complexity. By creating associations that take advantage of the dissolving boundaries between the fields of design, science, technology and the fine arts, RoTo has become a specialist in finding non-standard solutions to unconventional and unique problems. Michael Rotondi's work has been described by Charles Jencks as reflecting a 'cybernetic process of design' and having 'the qualities of a sketch: like the assemblage sculpture of the 1960s, it prefers vitality and function to visual completion. It is yet one more analogue of the city of Los Angeles in motion.'[2]

Notes

1   Michael Rotondi, statement to the author, February 1999
2   Charles Jencks, *Heteropolis: Los Angeles, the Riots and the Strange Beauty of Hetero-Architecture* (London: Academy Editions, 1993), p 61

Dorland Mountain Arts Colony

Temecula, California, 1994

1.31 This exploratory project consists of a pavilion intended as a hideaway for visiting artists in the Temecula Valley Nature Reserve. Its stylistic origins, including the choice of materials, systems and construction procedures, are deeply entrenched in an analysis of the relationship between nature and creativity. The architects draw on human innovation, viewed as a progressive system, and the transition of natural elements from one state to another, which they translate into the design of their buildings. Using alternative construction techniques to shape the volume and configure the forms, the project incorporates such elements as non-parallel planes and complex parabolic surfaces that reveal dynamic, kinetic features. There is scant use of conventional technology: electricity is deliberately treated as a scarce resource, in contrast to the customary assumption that it is limitless. In fact, the project has no electrical supply at all; the only source of energy is a small solar-panel system. Furthermore, special architectural features are incorporated, taking account of the limited heat supply. For reasons of economy, the entire building was designed to be built from local resources and was geared to an extremely simple assembly system. By eschewing overt and even standard technologies in the design and construction of the building, RoTo establishes a dialogue between found nature and man-made intervention, offering alternatives that suggest analogies to the process of creativity itself and mirror its logic in an unexpected way.

Carlson Reges Residence
Los Angeles, 1992–96

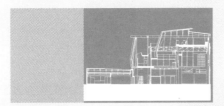

1.32 A startling reinterpretation of the machine, the house – formerly the machine shop of Los Angeles' first electrical station from the 1920s – is an amalgamation of parts literally scavenged from its site, a former industrial area near downtown. A steel-girder depot on the site yielded cast-off trusses, beams and staircases. Fundamental to the design was the subversion of the repetitive character of these industrial parts by reassembling them in non-standardized ways. To do this, RoTo drew on the contours of the surrounding landscape to create geometries that organized the recycled components. Its dramatic recombination of elements such as a horizontal, steel gas tank and various industrial components including glazing and decking units and exposed trusses and I-beams, presents an exuberant, raw muscularity that evokes both the memory of the site's dynamic past as an industrial setting abutting a railway yard and calls attention to its present-day revitalization as a live-work setting for artists and designers. A corrugated-metal shield was added to the railyard side of the house to mitigate sound and diesel fumes, creating a tall perimeter wall at grade. The result is a building that projects a tense state of ambiguity, wavering between the certainty of the old and the uncertainty of the new and displaying tectonic expression without being merely technological.

Warehouse C Exhibition Hall
and Public Gardens
Nagasaki, Japan, 1996–98

1.33 The inspiration behind a warehouse in Japan's Nagasaki Harbour comes from its situation among heavy machinery in the shipping industry. Approximating a piece of built topography, it responds to the character and configuration of its site on a new infill pier in this active harbour. A hulking shed-like building animated by a faceted form and a gently twisting profile, the warehouse is clad in a manner reminiscent of an ocean-going tanker with steel plates manufactured locally at the Mitsubishi shipyards and roofed in sail-like sheets of Teflon. On top of the warehouse is a public garden, where visitors can stroll as in a traditional 'dry garden', and where there is also an observation deck with views over the harbour. The roof zone contains a large red sphere intended as a space for public events. This dialogue between old and new, taking its cue from the history, identity and materiality of the site, highlights RoTo's characteristic emphasis on the interdependence of diverse components in the genesis of a building's design and on the application of a systematic logic that produces surprising and non-formulaic results.

Technology Building, Sinte Gleska University
Rosebud, South Dakota, 1993–99

1.34

In 1993, RoTo Architects began working in conjunction with the Lakota Nation to plan Sinte Gleska University, the first Native American college in the United States. The Technology Building consists of classrooms for teaching science, computer technology and more advanced media technology for 'distance learning'. Similar to the approach taken in all the buildings for Sinte Gleska University, RoTo's emphasis is on the integration of artifacts of mass production and modular building components with handicraft techniques. In the Technology Building RoTo combined a quintessentially American building system of off-the-shelf components, including a Butler building (a low-cost prefabricated steel shed), with handmade elements, highlighting contrasts and analogies between such methods and materials as steel framing and timber. The practice's goal has been to articulate the idea that human systems are only a subset of natural systems, and that our technologies, including building technologies, should be applied with a sense of balance and restraint. They have examined and responded to the problem of designing buildings in this context by studying the contemporary condition and finding links to traditional, organic and integrated systems of values, therefore connecting the social, the technological and the natural, which is the basis of an indigenous understanding of the universe.

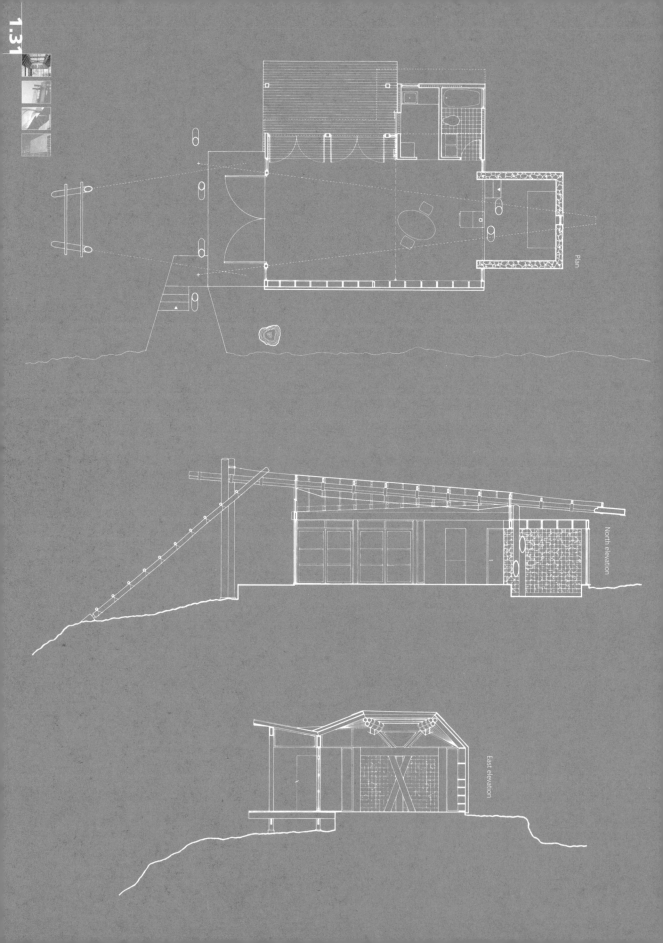

Plan

North elevation

East elevation

1.31 Arts Colony

At first glance the structure appears to be an ad-hoc shack thrown together by some dizzy mountain artists. A closer look reveals a carefully considered minimal shelter balancing the conditions of economy, practicality and remoteness by incorporating basic rustic construction techniques and mechanical procedures, locally available materials and the highest of high technology. Systems and materials are deployed pragmatically to address specific problems, for example, the high-tech nature of solar electric panels or translucent polyester fibre is no more or less important than nylon rope ties connecting telephone poles or wood-burning stoves.

1.32 Carlson Reges Residence
A hybrid entity is vividly fashioned from scavenged detritus, salvaged from the heart of industrial Los Angeles and incorporated into the derelict shell of a neoclassical power station. The building brings new meaning to the word contextual. A series of section drawings diagram the geometry of the existing power station and the new residence.

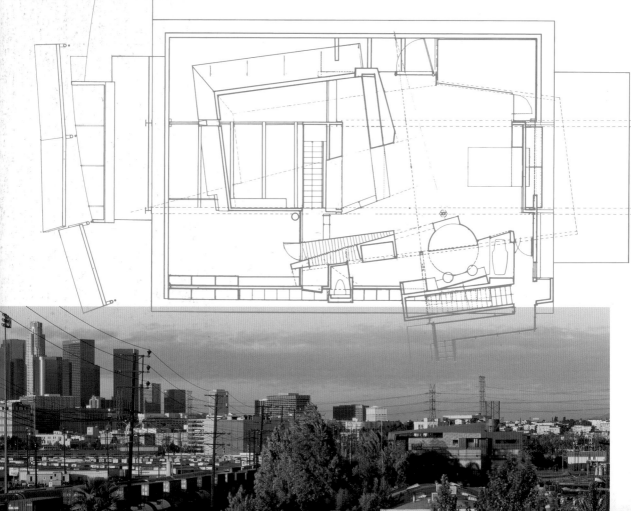

Third-floor plan

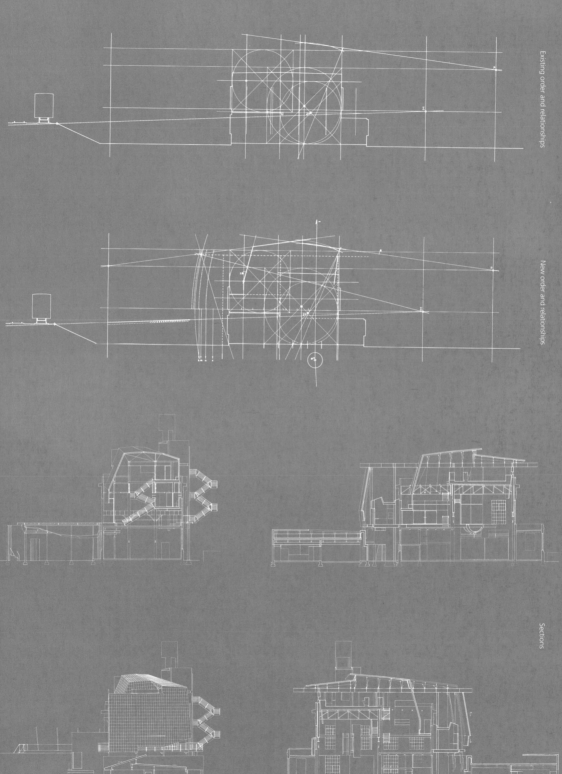

Existing order and relationships

New order and relationships

Sections

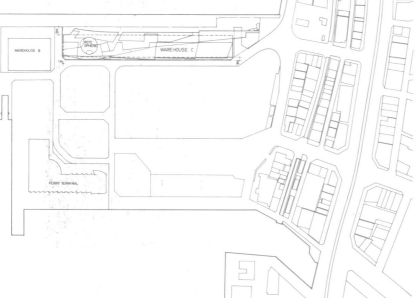

Site plan

WAREHOUSE B

ROTO SPHERE

WAREHOUSE C

FERRY TERMINAL

1.33 Warehouse C
The building presents a linear yet organic condition in response to its harbourside site. Gently twisting and rising to reflect surrounding industrial topography, it approximates an ocean-going tanker in scale, but avoids being monolithic.

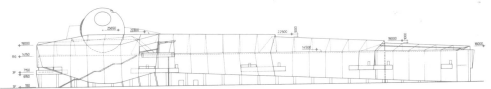

North elevation

South elevation

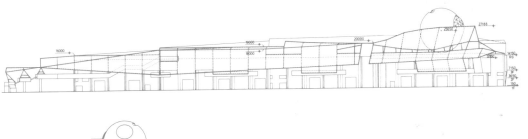

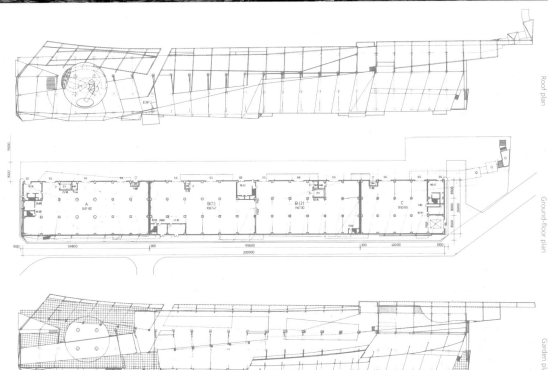

Roof plan

Ground-floor plan

Garden plan

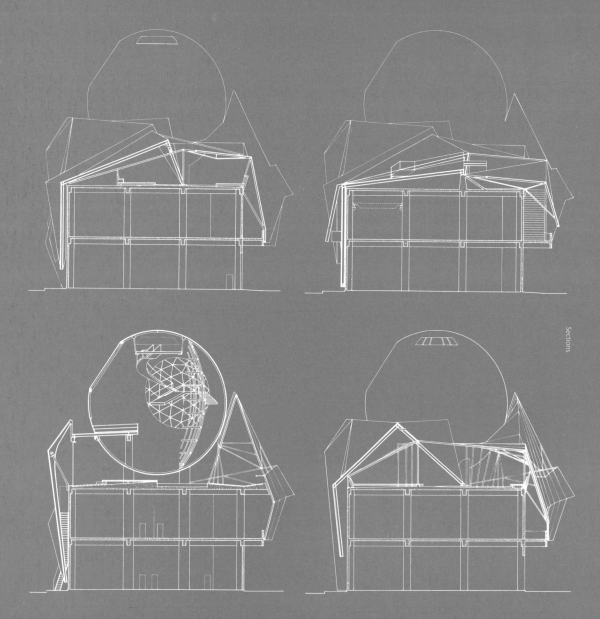

Sections

1.33 Warehouse C
The building's dynamism is more readily discernible from street level by means of its faceted profile, allowing points of observation to the city and harbour beyond. The section drawings show the extent of RoTo's additions to the existing warehouse: cladding and structural elements that shape the roof garden and surround the spherical dome.

貨物上屋
Storage Shelter

ルビル
Building

1.34 Technology Building
As seen from the exterior, the building is an amalgam of disparate components, materials and profiles yet its design is far from arbitrary. Its site was decided after a lengthy study and consideration of Lakota cosmology and a recognition that the genesis of the architecture was in the infinite variety offered by the landscape.

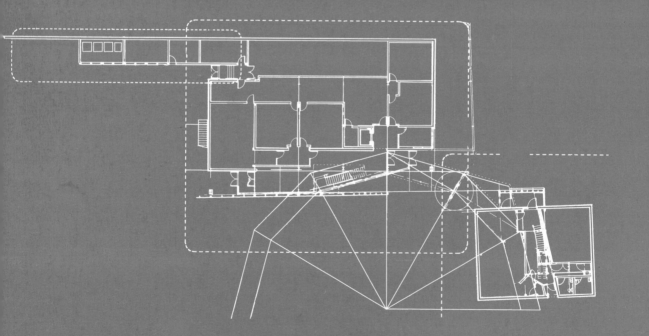

1.34 Technology Building
Conjoining open and closed
forms, handmade wood framing
elements and low-cost modular
building parts, the curvilinear
and the right-angled, the
building reflects an
improvisational sensibility and a
combinatorial process that
informs RoTo's own work yet
also clearly relates to the history,
traditions and contemporary
realities of the Lakota people.

Panel-roof plan

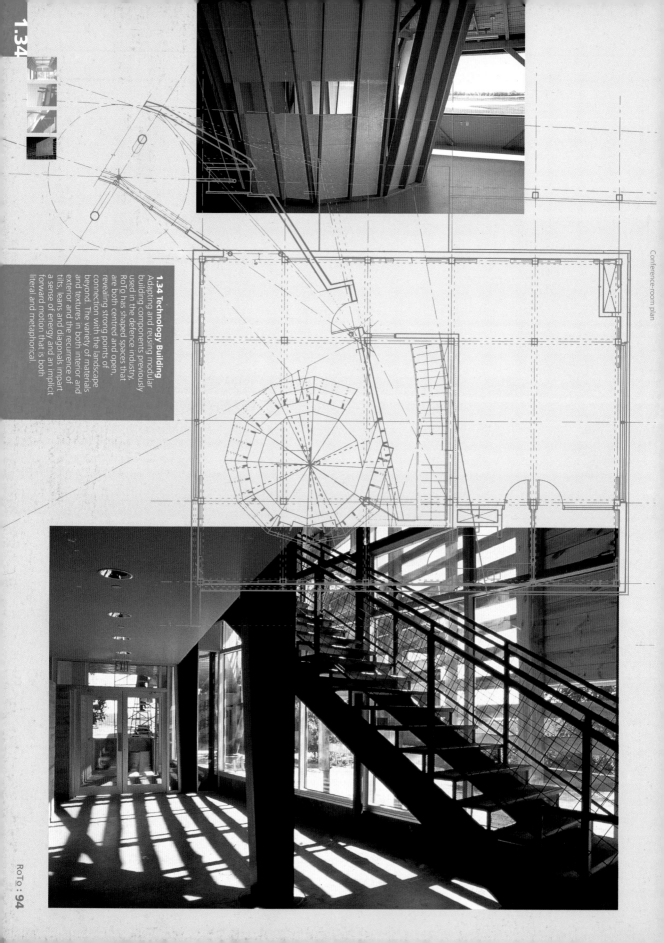

Conference-room plan

1.34 Technology Building
Adapting and reusing modular
building components previously
used in the defence industry,
RoTo has shaped spaces that
are both centred and open,
revealing strong points of
connection with the landscape
beyond. The variety of materials
and textures in both interior and
exterior and the recurrence of
tilts, leans and diagonals impart
a sense of energy and an implicit
forward motion that is both
literal and metaphorical.

Smith-Miller + Hawkinson
Technological Materialism

1.40 The work of Smith-Miller + Hawkinson focuses on technology's relationship to materiality and to history, exploring the changing cultural consequences of technology and incorporating it in geographic, historical and temporal relationships. Lightweight, elegant and minimal, the buildings reflect an interest in the theoretical and analytical implications of technology. Departing from the early modernist definition of technology as mechanical, Henry Smith-Miller and Laurie Hawkinson embrace a more comprehensive vision that includes recent digital developments and that expresses architecture's complex and changing relationship to society. They are particularly keen to concentrate on ways in which their architectural programme can be developed through innovative interpretations that give physical expression to these underlying motivations. Through their analyses and materially expressive investigations, they seek an architecture that is sensitive to contemporary cultural needs and ideas. Characteristically, the architects explore the use of technological and industrially inspired materials, aiming to bring them into a programmatic, active state.

Henry Smith-Miller cites, as a source of inspiration, Kenneth Frampton's analysis of a direction within contemporary architecture to 'ground architecture once again in structure, craft and the poetics of construction rather than in the gratuitous aestheticism of abstract form'. He comments, 'In a period during which it is often difficult to distinguish a courthouse from a museum, we are interested in the subtle variations of massing, materials and details that allow for the particularity of a project in a specific context to be communicated and experienced . . . When working a project, we examine the site not only for its topographic and tectonic conditions but also for its historical and social dimension . . . We are interested in all aspects of a project's development, from its first programme development to its occupation by constituents and future alteration.'[1]

Writer Catherine Ingraham has described Smith-Miller + Hawkinson's approach as follows, 'This politics of materiality is not simply, or even partially, about a clever use of materials. It is more cybernetic in the sense that certain material (cultural) properties are breached and things drift into the "wrong" place. Windows become floors and so on. An attenuated posture towards materials – literally the elongation or distortion of mass, volume, substance – is also a kind of tampering with their proper genetic domain.' Compounding this analysis by noting that the practice's work is predominantly 'an architecture of structures within structures where the building proper becomes host to, in some cases is taken over by, something suspended inside', Ingraham points to the penetrating way in which the architects 'handle the problem of the anomalistic, the internal stresses of working with non-linear genealogical structures, the add-ons and interstitial interventions.'[2]

Smith-Miller + Hawkinson, founded in 1977, is an architecture firm with offices in New York and Los Angeles. The practice consists of principals Henry Smith-Miller and Laurie Hawkinson. Its projects span small to very large and complex interiors and additions to freestanding single- or multi-use structures. Recent works and projects include the LaGuardia Airport Canopy (New York, 1990–92, p 100), 'Imperfect Utopia', the master plan and an addition to the North Carolina Museum of Art (Raleigh, 1987–93), the Corning Museum of Glass (Corning, 1997, p 101), the Wall Street Ferry Terminal Pier II (lower Manhattan, 1995–99), the Shilla Daechi Building for Samsung Corporation (Seoul, Korea, 1996–97, p 102) and numerous residential projects.

One of six American architecture firms, Smith-Miller + Hawkinson was invited to exhibit in the Italian Pavilion at the 1996 Venice Biennale and their work was included in the exhibition Urban Revisions: Current Projects for the Public Realm at The Museum of Contemporary Art, Los Angeles in 1995. A monograph on the practice was published by Gustavo Gili in 1994 and the firm was also included in the Michael Blackwood film New Modernists: Nine American Architects (1993).

Notes
1   Taken from an interview with Henry Smith-Miller, February 1999
2   Catherine Ingraham, Smith-Miller + Hawkinson (Barcelona: Editorial Gustavo Gili, 1995)

LaGuardia Airport Canopy
New York, 1990–92

1.41 The architects approached the design of a prototype canopy for Continental Airlines (now U.S. Air) from the point of view of materiality and its relationship to the programme. Researching the materials used in the construction of aeroplanes to come up with a solution for prefabricated parts that could be used as a cantilevered canopy, Smith-Miller + Hawkinson developed a composite structure called Kevlar – a carbonfibre material from the aerospace industry, laid over a Nomex core. Altogether sixty-six Kevlar shells were composed, enabling an economical construction solution. This lightweight, long-span canopy provides visual identification as well as information and light-filtration devices. A space truss spans the canopy, designed to support its own weight, as well as lighting and LED equipment. The canopy consists of nine trusses linked end to end, supported at 30-foot (9-metre) intervals by a triangular light of laminated glass. The cantilevered canopy created a space within a space, highlighting the activity of transaction and the relationship between agent and customer. Not only did Kevlar prove effective in conveying an airborne, streamlined character to the interior, but the incorporation of an LED information system was also intended to express the transitory nature of travel. Smith-Miller + Hawkinson's investigative procedure produced a new application of materials that had not previously been used architecturally and were derived from the study of aeroplane technology and racing sailboat construction.

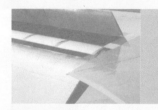

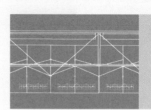

Corning Museum of Glass, PHASE ONE: West Bridge and Performing Arts Theater, 1997 and PHASE TWO: Orientation Center, 1999, Corning, New York

1.42

Smith-Miller + Hawkinson's addition offers a highly elegant and didactic use of glass, underscoring the history and identity of the building as well as providing a powerful visual and spatial element to it. Much like the first glass centre at the 1939 World's Fair, this building, originally designed by Wallace Harrison in 1951, represented an optimism about the future of industry and culture. Phase one of the project included the renovation of a performance space and the addition of a West Bridge, which serves as a lobby and connects different buildings on the site. In phase two, Smith-Miller + Hawkinson added a new orientation centre building to the east of the present glass centre. Accommodating pedestrians and jitney-borne visitors, the large glass façade of the orientation centre offers visual access to the interior, displaying the orientation theatre and the ramp leading to the exhibitions. To maintain maximum transparency, masts made up of high-tension stainless-steel members support the large frameless glass plates. Placement of the masts to the glass planes' interior and exterior and their linkage to the building's structure shifts the window wall from an element read as 'endoskeleton' to 'exoskeleton'. The use of glass is integral to the identity of the client, the client's industry and the existing building. Smith-Miller + Hawkinson's addition imparts a contemporary sensibility to the project while serving the programmatic needs of improving access to and understanding of the building's disparate components.

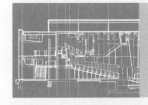

Shilla Daechi Building
Seoul, Korea, 1997

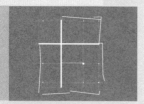

1.43

Responding to a district in the process of regeneration, this eight-storey office complex contains an exclusive fitness club and restaurant in the heart of the Kangnam area of Seoul. The client's desire to project an image of global consequence corresponds to Korea's newly found sense of worldwide awareness. The building's foremost feature is an exterior skin of titanium that functions as a symbolic advertisement for the building while providing visual protection. An interface between complex exterior forces and the collection of diverse interior programmes, the skin is a transitional element made up of overlapping planes and folds that confound the idea of conventional boundaries and defy the establishment of a clear perimeter in a manner evoking the shifting nature of the culture itself. It also recalls an important episode in Korean history when an admiral won an important sea battle against the Japanese by cladding his ship in an extra layer of armour that served as a protective skin. The craft became known as the 'Turtle Ship' – a name that Smith-Miller and Hawkinson have also used to describe their building. Double glazing used in the interior, intersecting and overlapping with the titanium skin, contrasts with the treatment of the ground plane, which appears more stable and solid. The project has undergone two design phases – the original design encompassed an automobile showroom on the ground floor and restaurants and conference rooms on the upper and lower floors.

House for a Film Producer,
Los Angeles, 1989–91, 1995–99

1.44 The design for extensions to the house challenges traditional compositional and formal design strategies. In lieu of fixed spaces and divisions, the transformable is considered; axiality is superseded by modality and the permanent is replaced with the temporary. The addition of a second storey and the intended alterations required removal and replacement of the house's structure, internalization of existing building openings and spaces and reinforcement of the existing spatial order. In a second phase of the design Smith-Miller + Hawkinson increased the building's amenities and spaces, further testing the idea of an 'additive and renegotiated' design to comment on aspects of the historical, geographical and economic circumstances of its location in Los Angeles. A hangar door within the house is a reminder of the defining moment in the early post-Second-World-War period (from when the original house, designed by a former associate of Richard Neutra, dates) in southern California and the prevalence of the defence and aerospace industries. Smith-Miller and Hawkinson chose a ready-made object, rather than developing a new material application to portray their interpretation of the history of California modernism. The design manifests the multiple conditions (cultural, economic, political and tectonic) inherent in the site and replaces the Eurocentric cultural focus of the original modernist design with a critical regionalist cultural sensibility.

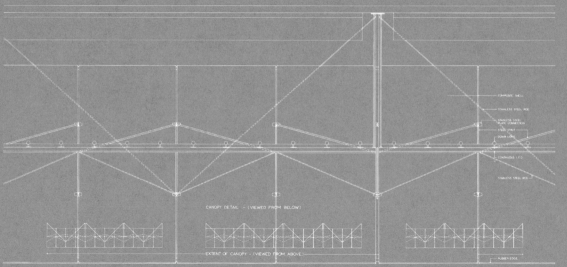

COMPOSITE SHELL

STAINLESS STEEL ROD

STAINLESS STEEL
PLATE CONNECTION

STEEL STRUT

DOWN LIGHT

CONTINUOUS L.E.D.

STAINLESS STEEL ROD

CANOPY DETAIL - (VIEWED FROM BELOW)

EXTENT OF CANOPY - (VIEWED FROM ABOVE)

RUBBER EDGE

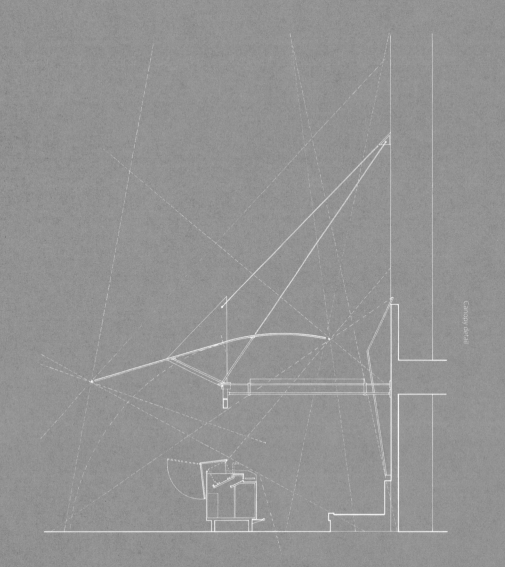

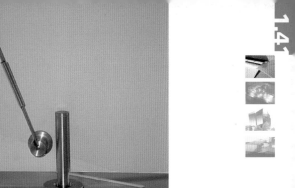

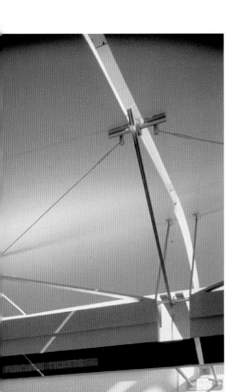

1.41 LaGuardia Airport Canopy
A section drawing overlaid with a diagram indicates axonometric relationships between the elements of the canopy and the existing terminal infrastructure. Clerestory windows allow natural light to activate the translucent qualities of the composite materials of the canopy.

1.41 LaGuardia Airport Canopy
Suspended from glass struts in tension, the thinness of the canopy belies its structural function of resisting a compressive load. The canopy itself, designed with the form of an aeroplane in mind, serves no utilitarian purpose. Instead, it mediates the cavernous scale of the terminal's volume, marks the intended location of the ticket counter within it, and communicates a sleek, cutting-edge image of its client.

West Bridge

Theater

Orientation Center

Gallery

Steuben Exhibition

Glass Museum

Steuben Factory/Offices

Retail

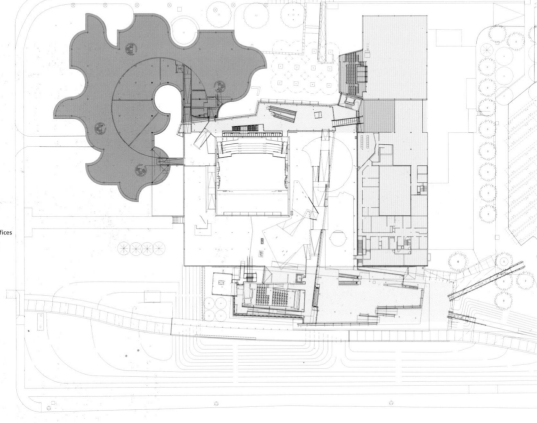

Ground-floor plan

Site plan

While Smith-Miller + Hawkinson's addition and remodel is relatively small in relation to the existing building, it is significant. The orientation centre, sheathed in glass, proudly displays the Corning company's product as its major component. Providing visual transparency, which assists visitors in locating their way and moving into and through the space, such an extensive use of glass also expresses its ability to blur the distinction between inside and outside.

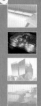

1.42 Corning Museum of Glass
Shifting the planar walls to rest at slight angles to each other enhances the faceted effect of the glass and provides an expressive counterpoint to the plastic sensuality of the curved glass of the museum building

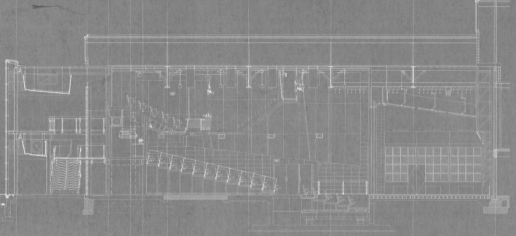

Auditorium cross section

Stairway detail

1.42 Corning Museum of Glass
The effect of consummate transparency is enhanced by the structural glazing system that does not employ integral mullions. Instead, steel fingers that rest on thin triangular plates at top and bottom gingerly 'hold' the glazing in place. The struts convey a sense of compression from holding up a heavy roof.

1.43 Shilla Daechi Building
The titanium-clad building is intended to dominate its site and serve as a beacon within its busy urban surroundings in a district described as being in a constant state of transformation and flux. Its interpenetrated volumes, best discernible at close range and in passage through the building, are derived from a complex set of spatial relationships meant to embody the idea of blurring traditional boundaries.

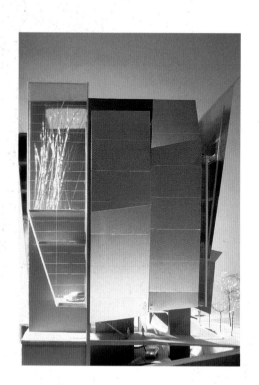

Plans

Wire-frame perspectives

1.44 House for a Film Producer
The original one-storey house formed the basis for a series of successive alterations including the addition of a second storey and the enlargement and opening up of several of the existing spaces. Circulation and skylight areas have been placed at the overlaps of the flat planes of the original building and the added planes, linking the upper and lower levels. A large wall at the north side of the stairs marks this operation and reinterprets the horizontal roof as a vertical plane.

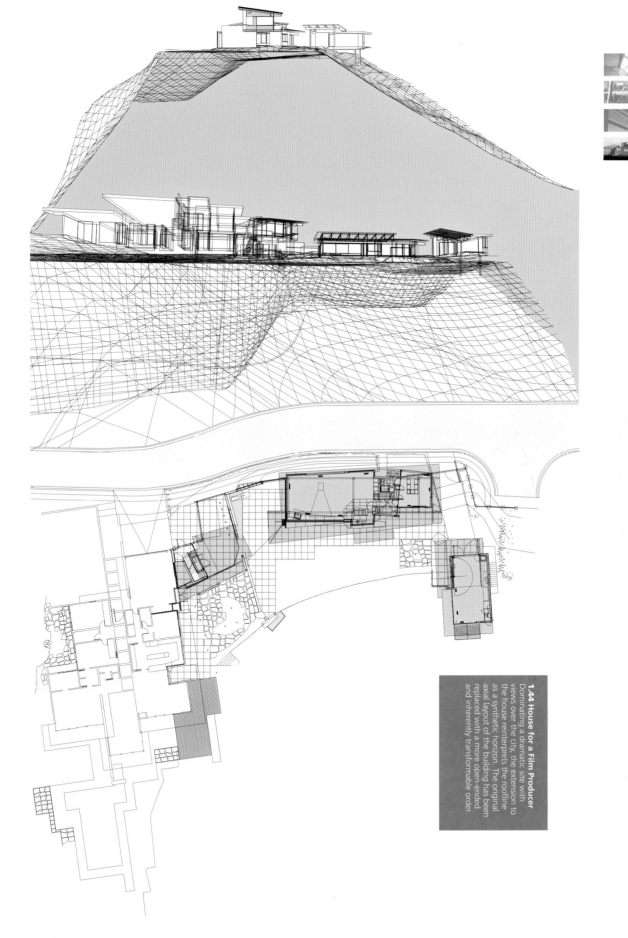

1.44 House for a Film Producer
Dominating a dramatic site with views over the city, the extension to the house reinterprets the roofline as a synthetic horizon. The original axial layout of the building has been replaced with a more open-ended and inherently transformable order.

Jones, Partners: Architecture

Biographical notes

Jones, Partners: Architecture was established in 1993 and has been based in El Segundo, California since 1997. Previously, Jones was Design Principal of the San Francisco–based office Holt Hinshaw Pfau Jones, during which time his work as partner in charge of design helped bring the firm to international prominence. Jones was educated at the University of California, Berkeley and at Harvard University's Graduate School of Design. Recipient of eight Progressive Architecture design awards, he is a former Fellow at the American Academy in Rome and a Graham Foundation scholar and has served as visiting professor at the universities of Harvard, Princeton, Rice, Tulane and Columbia.

Select bibliography

Adler, Jerr, 'Putting Names in the Sky', *Newsweek* (13 May 1989)

Award Issue, *Progressive Architecture* (January 1995)

Fisher, Thomas, 'Hot Rods', *Progressive Architecture* (September 1988)

——, 'Case Study: Holt Hinshaw Pfau Jones', *Progressive Architecture* (July 1991)

Futugawa, Yukio (ed.), 'Projects', *GA Houses* (no 34, 1990)

—— (ed.), 'Projects', *GA Houses* (no 37, 1991)

Georgiadis, Nikos, 'Tracing Architecture', *Architectural Design* (March–April 1998)

Hogben, Calvin, 'Mechanics', *The Architectural Review* (1987)

Jodidio, Philip, *Contemporary California Architects* (Cologne: Taschen Verlag 1996)

——, *New Forms* (Cologne: Taschen Verlag 1997)

Jones, Wes, 'The Hut and the Machine', *Transitions, Discourse on Architecture* (vol 4, no 3, 1983)

——, 'Holt Hinshaw Pfau Jones: Central Cogeneration Plant, San Jose Repertory Theater' *Zodiac* (March–April 1992)

——, 'Ideas and Approaches to Architecture and the City', *Space Design* (September 1992)

——, 'Central Cogeneration Plant', *A + U* (February 1996)

——, *Instrumental Form: Designs for Words, Buildings, Machines* (New York: Princeton Architectural Press 1998)

——, et al, 'Building; Machine', *Pamphlet Architecture* (no 12, 1985)

—— (guest ed.), 'The Mech In 'tecture: Reconsidering Materialism in the Electronic Era', *ANY* (Architecture New York, no 10, 1995)

Kliment, Stephen A., 'Cool Chiller', *Architectural Record* (June 1992)

Lacy, Bill and Susan deMenil, *Angels and Franciscans* (New York: Rizzoli 1990)

McCoy, Michael, 'Attitudes Toward Technology: Between Nature and Culture', *Progressive Architecture* (April 1989)

Mik, E., 'How Should Technology Manifest Itself in Architecture?', *Archidea* (Autumn 1991)

Muschamp, Herbert, 'Boss Design: A Los Angeles Sketchbook', *The New York Times* (12 June 1992)

'News', *Kenchiku Bunka* (June 1989)

'News', *Progressive Architecture* (January 1985)

'News', *Progressive Architecture* (January 1986)

'News', *Progressive Architecture* (January 1988)

Shay, James, *New Architecture San Francisco* (San Francisco: Chronicle Books 1987)

Sola-Morales, Ignaci and Xavier Costa (eds), *Present and Futures: Architecture in Cities* (Barcelona: Collegi d'Arquitectes de Catalunya 1996)

Project Information

UCLA Chiller Plant Facilities Complex
1990–94

Project team Dwight Ashdown, Sara Jane Chun, Paul Holt, Wes Jones, Scott Laidlaw, Jeff Logan, Mark Sparrowhawk

Client Ralph M Parsons Company and Kiewit Pacific Construction, for University of California

Consultant Parsons Main

Contractor Kiewit Pacific Construction

Photography Erich Ansel Koyama

Area 210,000 ft² (19,530m²)

Confluence Point Bridges and Ranger Station 1992–97

Project team Michael Gough, Paul Holt, Douglas Jackson, Wes Jones, Bob Shepherd, Robert Yue

Client Hargreaves Associates for The Redevelopment Agency of the City of San Jose

Consultants AN West (structural); GM Lim and Associates (mechanical)

Contractor B&B Construction, Garden City Construction

Photography Erich Ansel Koyama

Area 2.5 acres (1 hectare)

The Golden Plate, Union Square 1997

Project team Hendra Bong, Roberto Carabeo, Daniel Huh, Douglas Jackson, Jean Jones, Wes Jones, Ayako Mizushiro, Jim Rhee

Area 1 acre (0.4 hectares)

Brill Residence 1998–99

Project team Daniel Huh, Wes Jones, Jim Rhee, Steve Slaughter

Client Eric and Nanette Brill

Consultants Al Geller (structural); Sullivan Partnership (MEP)

Construction Shawn Delisio, B J Glidden (Jones, Partners: Architecture); Brian Kutza, Mike Nelms (Liquid Steel); Greg Abbott (Kleen Design); Stiener Brothers Construction

Photography Erich Ansel Koyama

Area 2400 ft² (223.2 m²)

TEN Arquitectos

Biographical notes

Enrique Norten was educated at the Universidad Iberoamericana in Mexico City and at Cornell University. He is a member of the Colegio de Arquitectos de Mexico, an advisor to the Urban Development Director for Mexico City and a founding member of the magazine *Arquitectura*. Norten was professor of architecture at the Universidad Iberoamericana from 1980–90 and has been a visiting professor at Parsons School of Design, Pratt Institute, University of Southern California, SCI-ARC (Southern California Institute of Architecture) and Rice University, among others. He currently holds the Miller Chair at the University of Pennsylvania, Philadelphia.

Bernardo Gómez-Pimienta was educated at the Universidad Anáhuac in Mexico City and Columbia University and is member of the Colegio de Arquitectos de Mexico and founding partner of the magazine *Arquine*. He was professor of architecture at the Universidad Iberoamericana, the Universidad Anáhuac and the Universidad Autonoma de Mexico, and visiting professor at SCI-ARC and the University of Illinois.

Select bibliography

Adria, Miguel (ed.), 'Taller de Enrique Norten Arquitectos', *Arquitectura* (October 1995)

——, *Mexico – 90s. Una Arquitectura Contemporanea* (Barcelona: Editorial Gustavo Gili 1996)

Asensio, Francisco (ed.), *New Architecture Eleven: Obra Reciente* (Barcelona: Editorial ARCO 1997)

Bossi, Laura, 'TEN Arquitectos', *Domus* (June 1996)

Carter, Brian (ed.), *The Work of TEN Arquitectos* (Ann Arbor: Michigan Architecture Press 1997)

Castaneda, Eduardo, et al, 'El Proyecto Arquitectonico de la Decada', *Revista Milenio* (August 1998)

Crombie, Edward, 'Dramatic Art', *The Architectural Review* (April 1995)

Dawson, Jessica Barrow, 'Project Portfolio, TEN Arquitectos', *Architecture* (March 1998)

Dorigati, Remo, 'Un'icona televisiva in Mexico City', *l'ARCA* (October 1996)

Fabrications (exhibition catalogue), The Museum of Modern Art, New York; San Francisco Museum of Modern Art; The Wexner Center for the Arts; and The Ohio State University. Essays by Aaron Betsky, Pat Morton, Terence Riley and Mark Robbins, (New York: The Museum of Modern Art 1998)

Frachon, Pierre, 'Atelier TEN', *L'architecture d'Aujourd'hui* (September 1993)

——, 'Televisa Mixed-Use Building', *GA Document* (no 50, April 1997)

Futugawa, Yukio (ed.), 'Enrique Norten – Drama Center', *GA Document* (no 44, August 1995)

—— (ed.), 'House Z, House LE', *GA Houses* (no 51, March 1997)

Gauza, Manuel (ed.), 'Enrique Norten. Casa LE', *Quaderns d'Arquitectura I Urbanisme* (no 213, Autumn 1996)

Giovannini, Joseph, 'Mexican Modern', *Architecture* (December 1996)

Gonzalez Gortazar, Fernando, *L'Arquitectura Mexicana del Siglo XX* (Mexico City: Consejo Nacional para la Cultura y las Artes 1994)

Hollein, Hans, *Sensori del Futuro. L'Architetto come Sismografo* (Milan: Electa 1996)

Ingersoll, Richard, 'Global Technics', *Architecture* (September 1995)

——, 'Mex-Tec Transmission', *Architecture* (December 1995)

——, 'Mexican Architecture at the End of the Millennium', *Lotus* (November 1996)

Ingersoll, Richard, Terence Riley and Michael Sorkin, *TEN Arquitectos: Enrique Norten – Bernardo Gómez-Pimienta* (New York: The Monacelli Press 1998)

Lee, WooJae (ed.), 'TEN Arquitectos', *Korean Architects* (no 143, July 1996)

Longoria, Rafael, 'After Barragán: Redefining Mexican Modernism', *Texas Architect* (September–October 1992)

Maurizio, Vitta, 'Cemento, acciaio e legno. House LE, Mexico City', *l'ARCA* (February 1997)

Moorhead, Gerald, 'Under Cabled Arches', *Architectural Record* (November 1994)

Noelle, Louise, 'Ondas anodizadas. Edificio de servicios para Televisa', *Arquitectura Viva* (March–April 1996)

Norten, Enrique, 'Immaterial Architecture', *Anybody* (Cynthia Davidson [ed.], Cambridge: The MIT Press 1997)

Perez Bodegas, Marisa (ed.), 'Casa LE en Ciudad de Mexico', *Diseno Interior* (February 1997)

Saslavsky, Ricardo (ed.), 'Centro de Arte Dramatico', *Enlace* (March 1997)

Seis años de arquitectura en Mexico (Mexico City: Universidad Nacional Autonoma de Mexico 1994)

Sola-Morales, Ignaci and Xavier Costa (eds), *Present and Futures: Architecture in Cities* (Barcelona: Collegi d'Arquitectes de Catalunya 1996)

'Televisa Mixed-Use Building', *Progressive Architecture* (January 1995)

Woods, Lebbeus, *TEN Arquitectos* (Barcelona: Editorial Gustavo Gili 1995)

Zellner, Peter, *Pacific Edge: Contemporary Architecture on the Pacific Rim* (London: Thames & Hudson and New York: Rizzoli 1998)

Project Information
National School of Theater 1993–94

Project team   Gustavo Espitia, Miguel Angel Gonzalez, Armando Hashimoto, Miguel Angel Junco, Carlos Valdez, Oscar Vargas

Client   The National Council for the Arts and Culture

Structural engineers Alonso-Garcia + Miranda

Mechanical engineer Tecnoproyectos

General contractors D.D.F. (Federal District Department); Francisco De Pablo (Dirección de Obras); Jesús Esteva (site engineer)

Acoustics   Jaffe, Scarborough & Holden

Computer model Alejandro de la Vega

Model   Jaime Cabezas, Gustavo Espitia

Photography Luis Gordoa

Area   108,000 ft² (10,000 m²)

Televisa Mixed-Use Building 1993–95

Project team   Raul Acevedo, Blanca Castañeda, Jesus Alfredo Dominguez, Héctor L. Gámiz, Rebeca Golden, Margarita Goyzueta, Javier Presas, Roberto Sheinberg, Maria Carmen Zeballos; Gustavo Espitia (site architect)

Client   Televisa S.A. de C.V.

Structural engineers Guy Nordenson (Ove Arup & Partners, New York); Colinas de Buen (S.A., Mexico)

Roof engineer Robert Harbinson (AMS Derby Inc.)

General contractors PYC, S.A.: Leopoldo Liberman (president) and Carlos César (site engineer)

Model   Jaime Cabezas, Gustavo Espitia

Photography Luis Gordoa, Armando Hashimoto

Area   81,000 ft² (7500 m²)

House LE 1994–95

Project team   Gustavo Espitia, Carlos Ordoñez

Structural engineer Colinas de Buen (S.A., Mexico)

Mechanical engineer Tecnoproyectos

General contractor Grupo Baia S.A.

Model   Jaime Cabezas, Gustavo Espitia

Photography Luis Gordoa

Area   3240 ft² (300 m²)

JVC Exhibition and Convention Center 1998–onward

Project team   Bernardo Gómez-Pimienta, Enrique Norten (principals); Julio Amezcua-Chazaro, Catalina Aristizábal, Diego Barberena, Jacques Cadhilac, Rubén Garnica, Carlos López, Claudia Marquina, Martine Paquin, Hugo Sánchez, Michael Shaw

Client   Jorge Vergara

Computer model Catalina Aristizábal, Jacques Cadilhac

Model   Miguel Ríos

Photography Luis Gordoa

Area   1,267,920 ft² (117,400 m²)

RoTo

Biographical notes

Michael Rotondi has been practising architecture for twenty-five years and has been a teacher for twenty-two years. He was one of the founders of SCI-ARC (Southern California Institute of Architecture) and was its director from 1987–97. A founding partner with Thom Mayne in the firm Morphosis (created in 1975), Rotondi worked on all kinds of projects both locally and internationally. Throughout his career he has been honoured with design awards: in 1992 he was a recipient of the American Academy Institute of Arts and Letters Prize for Architecture. The coupling of education and practice in his career has led to a flexible working method, integrating pure and applied research, the objective of which is to discover what is inevitable and unique about each project.

Clark Stevens was educated at the University of Michigan and Harvard University. He is a visiting faculty member of the graduate programme at SCI-ARC and in 1995 was named on the prestigious 'Forty under Forty' list, an honour given once a decade in a national competition.

Select bibliography

Buntrock, Dana, 'Port Authority', *Architecture* (August 1998)

Calmenson, Diane Weintraub, 'SCI-ARC's Collaborative Effort: Architecture and Education According to Michael Rotondi', *Interiors & Sources* (March 1997)

'Carlson Reges Residence', *Progressive Architecture* (May 1994)

Dixon, John Morris, 'The Santa Monica School', *Progressive Architecture* (May 1995)

'Dorland Mountain Arts Colony', *GA* (no 32, 1995)

Futugawa, Yukio and Wayne Fuji (eds), 'RoTo Architects', *GA Houses* (no 51, April 1997)

Giovannini, Joseph, 'L.A. Trouvée', *Zodiac* (1994)

——, 'The Future Pulls Into the Station', *The New York Times* (4 December 1997)

——, 'Transformations: Powered Up!', *Architecture* (February 1998)

Gubitosi, Allessandro, 'Artificio e natura: In the Temecula Valley', *l'ARCA* (February 1997)

Jencks, Charles, *Heteropolis: Los Angeles, The Riots and the Strange Beauty of Hetero-Architecture* (London: Academy Editions 1993)

Minetto, Renato, 'Architettura dell'Orientamento', *Abitare* (May 1997)

Moonan, Wendy, 'Designing Megahouses', *Architectural Record* (December 1998)

Morphosis: Buildings and Projects 1989–92 (New York: Rizzoli 1994)

'Nagasaki Port Warehouse C', *Space Design* (January 1996)

Reeve, Margi and Michael Rotondi (eds), *From the Center: Design Process at SCI-ARC* (New York: The Monacelli Press 1998)

ROTOBOOK: The Work of Michael Rotondi and Clark Stevens, essays by Michael Rotondi, Clark Stevens, Joseph Giovannini and Brian Carter (Ann Arbor: The University of Michigan 1996)

Rotondi, Michael, 'Visits, Meetings, Explorations', *Lotus* (1994)

'Rotondi: Dorland Mountain Arts Colony', *GA Houses* (no 46, 1994)

'RoToNDI: Carlson Reges House', *GA Houses* (no 37, 1993)

Ryan, Raymund, 'L.A. Rotation', *The Architectural Review* (October 1993)

——, 'Interdependence Day', *Blueprint* (June 1997)

Schrom, Georg, 'Gebäude lügen nicht . . . Michael Rotondi, Los Angeles', *Architektur Aktuell* (June 1995)

Stevens, Clark, 'Everyday Observations: Sinte Gleska University and RoT͟o Architects', *Architectural Design: The Everyday and Architecture* (Sarah Wigglesworth and Jeremy Till [eds], London: Architectural Design)

Toy, Maggie, *World Cities Los Angeles* (London: Academy Editions 1994)

'Warehouse C', *Nikkei Architecture* (February 1997)

'Warehouse C', *Nikkei Architecture* (May 1998)

'Warehouse C', *GA* (no 32, May–June 1998)

Project information

Dorland Mountain Arts Colony 1994

Project team   Michael Rotondi, Clark Stevens (partners in charge); Yusuke Obuchi (collaborator); Jim Bassett, Scott Francisco, Angela Hiltz, Brian Reiff, Jonathan Winton (project architects); Jin Kim, Kenneth Kim, Tracy Loeffler, Geoff Lynch, Caroline Spigelski, Joy Stingone, Michael Yeo (project assistants)

Client   Dorland Mountain Arts Colony

Associate architects   Rubb West / Azim Jessani, John McCoy

Consultants   April Greiman, John McCoy, Joseph Perazzelli

Photography   Assassi Productions

Area   1,000 ft² (93 m²)

Carlson Reges Residence 1992–96

Project team   Michael Rotondi, Clark Stevens (partners in charge); Angela Hiltz, Kenneth Kim, Yusuke Obuchi, Brian Reiff, Craig Scott (project architects); Michael Brandes, Peggy Bunn, Carrie Jordan, Bader Kassim, James Keyhani, Gregory Kight, Qu H. Kim, Thorsten Kraft, Tracy Loeffler, Lina Sipelis, Caroline Spigelski, James Malloch Taylor (assistant architects)

Clients   Richard Carlson, Kathy Reges

Consultants   April Greiman; Donald T. Griggs; David Mocarski (Arkkit-forms); Peter S. Higgins and Associates (structural); Richard Reyes (Live Load)

Photography   Tim Street-Porter, Assassi Productions (p 85)

Area   8300 ft² (771.9 m²)

Warehouse C Exhibition Hall and Public Gardens 1996–98

Project team   Michael Rotondi, Clark Stevens (partners in charge); Brian Reiff (collaborator); Max Massie, Michael Reck (project architects); Anthony Caldwell, James Keyhani, David Lazaroff, Jeannette Licari, James Malloch Taylor (project assistants)

Client   Nagasaki Prefecture, Japan

Associate architect   Arai Architects

Executive architect   Mitsubishi Estate Company

Consultant   April Greiman

General contractors   Eikawa Construction Company, Mitsubishi Heavy Industries, Taishin Construction Company, Taiyokogyo Corporation, Tanigawa Construction Company, Yoshikawa Construction Company

Photography   RoT͟o Architects

Area   Warehouse: 108,000 ft² (10,044 m²) Roof garden: 54,000 ft² (5022 m²)

Technology Building, Sinte Gleska University 1993–99

Project team   Michael Rotondi, Clark Stevens (partners in charge); Jim Bassett, Brian Reiff, Kenneth Kim, Michael Volk (collaborators); Noah Bilken, Martin Brunner, Marco Bruno, Carrie DiFiore, Carrie Jordan, Bader Kassim, Jarkko Kettunen, James Keyhani, Jin Kim, Qu H. Kim, John Maze, Michael McDonald, Craig Stewart, James Malloch Taylor, Gudrun Wiedemer, Susanna Woo (project architects)

Client   Lannan Foundation

Consultants   Bruce Biesman-Simons, April Greiman, John McCoy, Ove Arup & Partners, Joseph Perazzelli, Rosebud Sioux Reservation Community

General Contractor   Scull Construction, Shingobee Builders

Photography   RoT͟o Architects

Area   1,000 ft² (93 m²)

Smith-Miller + Hawkinson

Biographical notes

Henry Smith-Miller began a private practice in 1977, following a seven-year period with Richard Meier and Associates. He was educated at Princeton University and the Graduate School of Architecture at the University of Pennsylvania and received a Fulbright Grant to study architecture in Rome. He has held teaching positions at the universities of Virginia and Yale, and has also taught at Columbia University, Harvard University, the City University of New York and the University of Pennsylvania.

Laurie Hawkinson was educated at the University of California, Berkeley and Cooper Union. Currently an associate professor of architecture at Columbia University, she has also taught at SCI-ARC (Southern California Institute of Architecture), Harvard University, Yale University, Parsons School of Design and the University of Miami.

Select bibliography

Beck, Haig and Jackie Cooper, 'Multi-Purpose Building, Seoul, Korea: Smith-Miller + Hawkinson', *UME 5 Magazine* (1997)

Betsky, Aaron, 'Modern over Modern: House for a Film Producer', *Architectural Record / Record Houses* (April 1992)

——, 'An Enforced Minimalism: The Work of Smith-Miller + Hawkinson', *ARCHIS* (September 1997)

Bone, Kevin (ed.), *New York Waterfront* (New York: The Monacelli Press 1997)

'Canopy is Composites First Foray into Airport Architecture', *Advanced Composites* (September–October 1992)

'Continental Airline Facility', *I.D.* (The 38th Annual Design Review, July–August 1992)

Dollens, Dennis (ed.), 'Flight Time, A New Image Project for Continental Airlines', *Sites* (no 24, 1992)

Fabrications (exhibition catalogue), The Museum of Modern Art, New York; San Francisco Museum of Modern Art; The Wexner Center for the Arts; and The Ohio State University. Essays by Aaron Betsky, Pat Morton, Terence Riley and Mark Robbins, (New York: The Museum of Modern Art 1998)

Frampton, Kenneth (ed.), *American Masterworks: The Twentieth Century House* (New York: Rizzoli 1995)

'Henry Smith-Miller and Laurie Hawkinson', *La Biennale di Venezia* (Milan: Electa 1996)

Ingraham, Catherine, *Smith-Miller + Hawkinson* (Barcelona: Editorial Gustavo Gili 1995)

Muschamp, Herbert, 'Heroic Spaces and the Perfect Spoon', *The New York Times* (September 1997)

——, 'The Corning Glass Center: Where Innovators Have Captured the Aura of Glass', *The New York Times* (14 June 1998)

'Next Generation in New York: Smith-Miller + Hawkinson', *Space Design* (April 1996)

Ojeda, Oscar Riera (ed.), *The New American House* (New York: The Whitney Library of Design 1995)

—— (ed.), *The New American House 2* (New York: The Whitney Library of Design 1998)

'Project: Double-Skinned Building', *ANY* (Architecture New York, 17 January 1997)

'Rethinking the Present: House for a Film Producer, Beverly Hills, Los Angeles, California', *Arquitectura* (October 1991)

'Seoul Searching', *Blueprint* (April 1997)

'Smith-Miller + Hawkinson at the Architectural League', *Oculus* (December 1996)

Stephens, Suzanne, 'Currents: Before Boarding, Please Pass Beneath the Wing', *The New York Times* (23 July 1992)

Vogel, Carol, 'Western Civilization', *The New York Times Magazine* (9 December 1991)

Young, Lucie, 'Remodeling Utopia', *Metropolis* (March 1992)

Project information

LaGuardia Airport Canopy 1990–92

Project team	Laurie Hawkinson, Henry Smith-Miller (partners in charge); Eric Cobb (project manager); Jennifer Beningfield, Kevin Cannon, John Conaty, Paul Davis, Wanda Dye, Anne Hindley, Robert Holton, Ferda Kolatan, Alexis Kraft, Oliver Lang, Ellen Martin, Maria Ibanex de Sendadiano, Eric van der Sluys, Flavio Stigliano, Irina Verona
Client	Continental Airlines
Consultant	Lippincott & Margulies
Engineer	Guy Nordenson (Ove Arup & Partners)
Photography	Paul Warchol

Corning Museum of Glass
Phase 1: 1997, phase 2: 1999

Project team	Henry Smith-Miller (partner in charge); Laurie Hawkinson (principal); Ingalill Wahlroos (project manager); John Conaty, Ferda Kolatan, Oliver Lang (project design); Jennifer Benningfield, Paul Davis, Anne Hindley, Robert Holton, May Kooreman, Alexis Kraft, Ellen Martin, Eric van der Sluys, Maria Ibanez de Sendadiano, Joern Truemper, Irina Verona (project assistants)
Client	Corning Incorporated
Landscape architect	Quennell Rothschild Associates
Consultants	Associated Construction Consultants; Claude Engle Lighting Design; R. A. Heintges Architects; TriPyramid
Contractor	Ciminelli Construction
Engineers	Hunt Engineers & Architects (civil); Ove Arup & Partners (structural / MEP)
Photography	Paul Warchol, Michael Moran (p. 109)

Shilla Daechi Building 1997

Project team	Laurie Hawkinson, Henry Smith-Miller (partners in charge); John Conaty (project manager); Ferda Kolatan, Oliver Lang, Flavio Stigliano (project

architects); Catherine Bird, Kevin Cannon, Maria Ibanez de Sendadiano, Kwang-Soo Kim, Ellen Martin, Virginia Navid, Nam-ho Park; Ferda Kolatan, Oliver Lang (visualization)

Area	120,000 ft² (11,110 m²)

House for a Film Producer
1989–91, 1995–99

Project team	Laurie Hawkinson, Henry Smith-Miller (partners in charge); Starling Keene (design development); Alexis Kraft (project architect); Margi Glagovic Nothard (concept design); Wanda Dye, Ferda Kolatan, Keith Krumwiede, Oliver Lang, Christian Lynch
Consultants	Steven Mezey & Associates (structural); Helfman/ Haoosim (mechanical); Achva Benzinberg Stein (landscape)
Contractor	Archetype
Area	7500 ft² (695 m²)
Photography	Paul Warchol

Illustration credits

(pp 1–23) **Frontmatter**: p 1 UCLA Chiller Plant (Jones, Partners: Architecture); p 2 Confluence Point (Jones, Partners: Architecture); p 3 National School of Theater (TEN Arquitectos); p 4 JVC Exhibition and Convention Center (TEN Arquitectos); p 5 Technology Building (RoTo); p 6 Carlson Reges Residence (RoTo); p 7 Corning Museum of Glass (Smith-Miller + Hawkinson); p 8 LaGuardia Airport Canopy (Smith-Miller + Hawkinson); p 9 Corning Museum of Glass (Smith-Miller + Hawkinson); p 10–11 UCLA Chiller Plant (Jones, Partners: Architecture); **Introduction**: p 14 John Edward Linden Photography; p 16 Shunji Ishida, Courtesy of Renzo Piano Workshop; p 17 From the Collections of Henry Ford Museum & Greenfield Village; p 18 S. Mills, Courtesy of Eames Office; p 19 Drawing Courtesy of Eames Office; p 20 Courtesy of L'Association de Amis de la Maison de Verre; p 21 Luis Gordoa; p 23 Courtesy of L'Association de Amis de la Maison de Verre

---

Cover design: *background image* Corning Museum of Glass (Smith-Miller + Hawkinson); *front, from top* UCLA Chiller Plant (photograph by Luis Gordoa), Carlson Reges Residence (photograph by Assassi Productions), Corning Museum of Glass; *back, from top* Brill Residence (photograph by Erich Ansel Koyama), National School of Theater (photograph by Luis Gordoa), Technology Building (photograph by RoTo), Corning Museum of Glass (photograph by Michael Moran); *back flap, from top* UCLA Chiller Plant (photograph by Erich Ansel Koyama), Televisa Mixed-Use Building (photograph by Luis Gordoa), Warehouse C (photograph by RoTo), House for a Film Producer (photograph by Paul Warchol); *inside cover, front* Corning Museum of Glass (Smith-Miller + Hawkinson); *inside cover, back* LaGuardia Airport Canopy (Smith-Miller + Hawkinson, photograph by Paul Warchol)

First published in the United Kingdom in 2000 by Thames & Hudson Ltd, 181A High Holborn, London WC1V 7QX

British Library Cataloguing-in-Publication Data
A catalogue record for this book is available from the British Library

ISBN 0-500-28232-3

Printed and bound in China by Everbest Printing Co. Ltd.